MURDER, INTERRUPTED

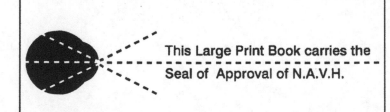

This Large Print Book carries the
Seal of Approval of N.A.V.H.

MURDER IS FOREVER

MURDER, INTERRUPTED

TRUE-CRIME THRILLERS

JAMES PATTERSON
WITH ALEX ABRAMOVICH
AND CHRISTOPHER CHARLES

THORNDIKE PRESS

A part of Gale, a Cengage Company

GALE
A Cengage Company

Farmington Hills, Mich • San Francisco • New York • Waterville, Maine
Meriden, Conn • Mason, Ohio • Chicago

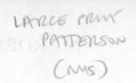

LARGE PRINT
PATTERSON
(NMS)

478 Gale J

Copyright © 2018 by JBP Business, LLC.
Investigation Discovery and the ID Investigation Discovery logo are trademarks of Discovery Communications, LLC.
Thorndike Press, a part of Gale, a Cengage Company.

LIBRARY OF CONGRESS CIP DATA ON FILE.
CATALOGUING IN PUBLICATION FOR THIS BOOK
IS AVAILABLE FROM THE LIBRARY OF CONGRESS

ISBN-13: 978-1-4328-5310-5 (hardcover)

Published in 2018 by arrangement with Grand Central Publishing, a division of Hachette Book Group, Inc.

Printed in Mexico
1 2 3 4 5 6 7 22 21 20 19 18

Dear Reader,

Above all else I'm a storyteller. I craft stories for insatiable readers. And though my books may seem over-the-top to some, I find that I am most often inspired by real life. After all, truth is stranger than fiction.

The crimes in this book are 100% real. Certain elements of the stories, some scenes and dialogue, locations, names, and characters have been fictionalized, but these stories are about real people committing real crimes, with real, horrifying consequences.

And as terrifying and visceral as it is to read about these crimes gone wrong, there's something to remember: *the bad guy always gets caught.*

If you can't get enough of these true crimes, please watch the pulse-racing new television series on Investigation Discovery, *Murder Is Forever,* where you'll see these shocking crimes come to life.

I hope you're as haunted by these accounts as I am. They'll remind you that though humans have the capacity for incredible kindness, we also have the capacity for unspeakable violence and depravity.

JPatterson

CONTENTS

CONTENTS

■ ■ ■ ■

MURDER,
INTERRUPTED

JAMES PATTERSON
WITH ALEX ABRAMOVICH

■ ■ ■ ■

PROLOGUE

August 2012

The .380-caliber bullet ripped through her left eye and down through the roof of her mouth on its way to her lung, where it lodged, hard up against her rib cage.

Spinning, she fell to the floor.

There was so much blood. So much blackness.

She slumped and a minute went by. Then, an honest-to-goodness miracle happened: The woman came to her senses and heard God's own voice, lifting and pulling her through.

"Get up," the voice said. "Get up, Nancy. Get *up!*"

Even though she was in shock and grievously wounded, she suddenly knew where she was: lying on the concrete floor of a garage. The garage of a house — her own home — on Bluebonnet Way, in a posh Dallas suburb where only the paranoid locked their front doors and all of her neighbors treated each other's kids as their own.

The woman knew *who* she was: Nancy Howard, aged fifty-three.

A loving wife. A churchgoer. Above all, a doting mother.

She *had* to live, for the sake of her kids.

Nancy knew it was August: The concrete felt heavy and warm. And although the floor was slippery with her blood, she started crawling.

"How could this happen?" she said to herself. "Sweet Jesus, how is this happening? And why is it happening to *me*?"

She needed her phone now to call 911. But her phone was in the purse taken by the man who had shot her.

Left for dead, she was still breathing, although with each breath it got harder and harder. And so she crawled, and as she crawled she thought, *My car is here, in the garage.*

The car has OnStar.

The OnStar operator can call 911.

Somehow, she managed to open the door. But without her key, which was in her stolen purse, OnStar would not turn on.

"Oh, Jesus, help me," she said. "Jesus, just give me the strength to stand up!"

■ ■ ■ ■

PART ONE:
DECEMBER 2011

■ ■ ■ ■

CHAPTER 1

Frank and Nancy

Christmastime was approaching in Carrollton, Texas, and Nancy Howard's husband, Frank, was putting up the Christmas lights.

The two-story brick house was the sort of house Frank and Nancy had dreamed about since the day they were married, twenty-eight years ago now, in Frank's daddy's church. The house where their three grown-up children always came back to for the holidays.

Nancy missed Ashley, Jay, and Brianna so much it was like part of her own body had gone missing. But the truth was that she also looked forward to her years as an empty nester. Frank was a hardworking man. At home he'd been a devoted father, with all the time in the world for their kids. Nancy loved and admired those qualities. But Frank's work, the kids, and all of the hours that Nancy and Frank had spent with their church — that meant less alone time for them. Hard as it was to see her children leave home, Nancy looked for a silver lining and found one: In all of the months and years to come, she'd have more of Frank to herself.

At least, that's what Nancy had thought.

The Howards had seen each other through some hard times. Ashley, their oldest, had barely survived her first days in the hospital. That had tested Frank and Nancy's faith. So had Frank's prostate cancer and Nancy's fibromyalgia — a chronic condition that disturbed her sleep and her moods and made her muscles ache constantly. But in the end, those trials had only strengthened their bond.

Then, in 2009, Frank's two-man accounting firm had taken on a new client.

At first, it had seemed like a windfall. The client was a defense contractor named Richard Raley — a man with significant interests in the Middle East. What Raley did specifically was ship ice, military hardware, and other equipment to American troops in Iraq. What he'd engaged Frank to do, after the death of his previous accountant, was to help him manage tens of millions of dollars he'd made in Kuwait.

Officially, Frank was to be paid $10,000 a

month to advise Raley's firm on issues relating to investments and taxes.

Frank had his questions about the operation, and about Richard Raley, but he kept them to himself, and Raley ended up making Frank his chief financial officer.

The job came with significant perks: new office space, the use of Raley's own private jet. Frank bought himself a Lexus and began flying to the West Coast, Europe, and the Middle East on business. Left behind in Carrollton, Nancy felt lonely and abandoned. But what made it worse was that the Frank who came back from these trips seemed less and less like the man she had married.

Distant. Furtive. Angry.

For two years now, those were the words Nancy had tried to avoid when she thought of her husband.

For two years, those same words kept coming to mind.

Nancy blamed Richard Raley and the long hours that Frank had been putting in, ever since Raley had made him his CFO. Frank himself had told her that the job was wearing him out. But Nancy wondered if there was more to it than that. Something she couldn't put her finger on. Something that was nagging at Frank and pulling him further and further away from their marriage.

Now she watched from the kitchen as Frank dug around in a big bin of old holiday decorations.

After a minute, he pulled out something that looked a lot like a strongbox.

Furtively, he carried the box out into the yard.

Outside, Frank darted behind a bush and dropped the strongbox into a small hole he'd dug there. In the time that it took Nancy to follow him into the yard, he'd made it back up the ladder.

"Frank? *Frank*?"

Jesus, Frank thought, *what is it now?*

"These are all wrong," Nancy said, pointing at the Christmas lights he'd already strung up. "You're going to do this side *over.*"

Looking down from the ladder, Frank smiled. But underneath he was seething. As far as he was concerned, Nancy nagged him and nagged him, always over the smallest details. But the big picture was completely beyond her. She simply couldn't see how hard Frank had worked for their family. She couldn't understand the sacrifices he'd made, all his traveling, his long hours. And when he got home, there she was — always nagging and egging him on.

Who *cared* if the Christmas lights were crooked?

Frank barely swallowed his fury.

"Well, if you say so!" he said as he adjusted the lights.

CHAPTER 2

Frank

Frank Howard had always been proud that he was born and raised a preacher's kid. He met Nancy in his father's church in San Marcos — when they got married in that same church, Frank's father performed the ceremony himself — and here in Carrollton, their Baptist church was the center of their social life. Frank and Nancy took part in the church's community outreach programs. They prayed for international missionaries and for poor people closer to home. They sang in First Baptist's choir. And they gave very freely to the church.

A few days before Christmas, the Howards' minister pulled them aside after choir rehearsal to thank them for the truly remarkable donation they had just made.

"Well," Frank told the minister, "the Lord's blessed me with so many incredible opportunities."

"It wouldn't be right not to share our good fortune with others," Nancy added.

Moments like these made Nancy thankful for Frank's job. Giving to others reminded of her of how much she herself had been given. Blushing slightly, she thought of the good things that the past few years had brought their family. Nancy knew that for Frank, gaining Raley as a client had been the start of a whole new life.

In point of fact, it had been the beginning of *two* new lives. A richer, more rewarding life here in Texas. And a life on the West Coast that Nancy knew nothing about and would have been shocked to discover.

But what Nancy didn't know wouldn't hurt her — at least not today, as she smiled at the minister and all of the nice things the minister said.

"You know, I'm *still* just a preacher's kid from downstate," Frank said as the minister wrapped up his song of praise and gratitude. Turning to the minster's wife, he added, "Who knows, if things hadn't turned out differently in my life, I could have ended up with a church of my own. But Nancy and I love it here at First Baptist. We're so happy to give back. And, truly, it's no big thing. Just the way my daddy raised me."

The four of them stood there silently.

Maybe even a bit awkwardly. Then the minister's wife turned to Nancy.

"Won't it be nice," the wife said, "to have all your chicks coming back to their nest?"

"Heaven!" said Nancy. "You know, it'll be like paradise, right here on Earth."

She was beaming now as Frank took her hand and stood, smiling, beside her.

CHAPTER 3

The Howards

On Christmas Eve the whole Howard family — Frank and Nancy, Ashley, Jay, and their youngest, Brianna — gathered in front of the fire. It was a family tradition, and this was a special year. Their family was about to get bigger. Brianna had brought her fiancé, Jed, along, and Nancy couldn't stop oohing and aahing over the engagement ring that Jed had bought for her daughter.

"How did you and Frank meet?" Jed asked.

Nancy loved to tell this story: Frank's daddy's church in San Marcos. Falling in love with the minister's kid. It had made perfect sense at the time — Nancy herself was the daughter of a church pianist in Driftwood — and Nancy still remembered how handsome Frank looked, with that crooked smile of his and his thick shock of black hair. She loved to talk about how they fell in love

23

across the pews and tied the knot in that very same church.

She'd just gotten to the part about the pews when Frank's phone started to ring.

"Work," he whispered.

"On Christmas Eve?" Nancy whispered back.

"I have to take it," Frank said, loudly enough to catch Ashley's attention.

"What's happening?" she asked. "Daddy, what is it?"

"Nothing, sweetie. I'll be back in a moment."

With Frank gone, Nancy tried to pick the thread of her story back up: Frank's father's church. Falling in love across the pews. But all the emotions that she'd felt rising up in her just a moment ago fell as flat as a collapsed soufflé. She stumbled on her own words. And when Frank returned, he broke the bad news to the whole room at once: The call was from his boss, who needed a new account set up and needed it done before New Year's.

It was important work. Work that would not wait.

"No!" Nancy said. "Flying out on *Christmas*? Just say no, Frank! Who works on Christmas *Day*, anyway? Don't you have any backbone at all?"

Frank made the usual appeals. First, he played the part of the patriot: "Those boys in Iraq that we work for — they don't take Christmas off. They're laying down their lives for us every day, making the *hard* sacrifices."

Then Frank played the part of the victim. Brought up the sacrifices *he'd* made — sacrifices that he *continued* to make — for the troops, for Nancy, for the kids: "You think I *want* to be traveling on Christmas? My whole life is here, in front of this fireplace. Who else would I even be doing this for?"

Frank teared up a bit, thinking about all he'd done for his family. His voice broke, twice, as he talked, and Nancy's heart broke to hear him. Duly chastised, she dried her own tears, apologized, and felt bad for feeling so selfish — for wanting Frank all to herself — when all *he* wanted to do was take care of them. Looking at him now, she really did understand how hard Frank had been working. How tiring all of this traveling must be. How much he'd given up for his family. All those late nights at the office. All of those trips out of town.

By the time Frank was done talking, she'd fallen in love with him all over again.

CHAPTER 4

Frank and Suzanne

It was Christmas Day in Santa Cruz, California, and Suzanne Leontieff had been waiting — forever, it seemed — for her lover to walk to her door, take her in his arms, and . . . and *what*?

Standing there in her lace nightgown, Suzanne blushed just thinking about it.

She was middle-aged now but more attractive than most women half her age. A true born-and-bred California girl, blond as the best of them, smart, self-assured. She had a good, solid job as a dental hygienist. Daughters as beautiful as she had been when she was their age. And Suzanne's lover was attractive too. Wealthy, and with a full head of hair that had only just begun to go gray at the temples.

Suzanne thought it made him look dignified rather than old.

The two of them had met a few years

previously, at a softball tournament in Tahoe. Both of Suzanne's daughters played softball at the tournament level. She was forever ferrying them to tournaments. But in Tahoe she'd decided to take some time for herself. After another long day out in the bleachers, she'd wandered into a lakeside casino. There, at one of the tables, she'd met the man she would fall for — a man who would sweep her away.

They gambled together for a night, flirted, and, finally, parted. But the attraction was undeniable.

"It's too bad you're married . . . ," Suzanne said, and stared at him meaningfully.

A part of her had to have known that once she said it out loud, there'd be no going back.

That part of her had been right.

They met the next day, and the day after that. Suzanne was separated from her own husband. Now the man she'd suddenly fallen for told her that his own marriage had taken a turn for the worse.

It wasn't long until the man, who was now her lover, was paying for tournament trips. He paid the college tuition for one of Suzanne's daughters. He bought Suzanne a new house in Santa Cruz — the house she was pacing around in now as she waited for him to arrive. The house had cost close to a million dollars. But her lover had paid in cash, then bought another home — a luxury condominium that they could share in Tahoe.

Suzanne's lover took her to exclusive restaurants, bought tickets to sold-out sporting events, flew her and the girls to the West Indies for a vacation.

He'd even started an IRA in Suzanne's name, depositing $700,000 of his own money.

This was not why she had fallen in love with the man. But, to be brutally honest, none of it had hurt his chances.

And now here he was. Ringing her doorbell. Holding an expensive bouquet and beaming.

CHAPTER 5

Frank

The flight from Texas had hollowed Frank out. The man sitting next to him in the fifth row was wearing an LSU sweatshirt, snakeskin shoes, and just about the amount of cologne it would take to drown a mama cat and all of her kittens.

It was a blessing that the good old boy hadn't talked all that much.

Frank no longer liked to fly commercial. The talk from other passengers made his head spin; the food made his bowels hurt; the stewardesses treated him (or so he felt) like a baby. When he was lucky enough to drift off, he dreamed of driving through the very same landscape — that long drive from Texas to California, with pit stops in Santa Fe, Tucson, Los Angeles. But there never was time enough for the drive, and Richard Raley's private plane was a luxury, not a day-to-day thing he could use whenever Suzanne sank into one of her *moods*.

"*Frank,*" she would say. "You said you would leave her. But here we all are!"

The way Frank figured it, he'd spent millions of dollars on the woman. The least she could do was be grateful. But, of course, some part of Frank knew she *was* grateful. She missed him was all, and was lonely for him. And when she opened the door in that lace nightgown that Frank had bought her, Frank was grateful too.

Together, they moved through the house. It was as if they were dancing. From the entryway to the living room. From the living room to the staircase. Then up the stairs to the bedroom, with Suzanne whispering in his ear the whole way.

"Frank," she said, in that low, sultry voice she used when she was feeling seductive. "Oh, Frank, the things that I'm going to *do* to you."

It was dark and they were naked and spent, drinking champagne in the bedroom, when Frank reached over, stuck his hand deep in the pocket of his black Burberry coat, and pulled out a baby-blue jewel box.

The box was small and wrapped with a ribbon, just the right size for a ring.

Suzanne squealed when she saw it. She

tore off the ribbon. And then her face dropped.

"Baby, they're diamonds," Frank said. "You don't like 'em?"

"They're perfect," Suzanne said, and managed a smile.

"You were expecting a ring?"

"Years, Frank. It's been years. How much longer am I supposed to wait?"

"I'm here, aren't I? Here, on Christmas, in the house that I bought for you. Can't you just wait a bit longer?"

He flashed the same smile that got to her back in Tahoe and she couldn't help but smile back. It really was Christmas. He really was here, and not back in Texas with *her*.

"Yes," Suzanne said.

"Promise?"

"I'm yours. And don't ever forget it."

The next day they drive to a casino. Suzanne forgets herself there, flirts with two men at the blackjack table, and ignores Frank until the moment her chips are all gone, at which point she asks him for another $10,000.

Frank nods to the floor manager. A moment later, new stacks of chips appear in front of Suzanne. But Frank's smile is as tight as it was in Texas, when Nancy was nagging him about those Christmas lights that he should have paid someone else to hang — and as he walks away from the table, that smile turns into something twisted.

Outside the casino, Frank pulls out a disposable cell phone — a burner — and punches out a short text.

Need to see you, he writes. *SOON. Next week. I'll drive out to your town.*

CHAPTER 6

Billie Earl Johnson

Frank's text from Tahoe caught Billie Earl Johnson passed out on the couch.

Billie's girlfriend, Stacey, was passed out beside him, snoring loudly, stirring slightly with each snore. Off in the corner, a hound dog whimpered away.

All in all it was just another Christmas in Ben Wheeler, an East Texas town that was as methed out as Carrollton was manicured.

In Ben Wheeler, Christmas might as well have been any old day of the week.

At rest, Billie's face was sunken and skull-like. Every crease was a physical record of years of hard living, hard drinking, and hard drugging. His slumped-over body was tattooed and sinewy.

Stacey's was tattooed and plump.

But as soon as he woke up, Billie's face took on a much harder edge.

The couch they had passed out on was

33

tatty and stained. The wood-paneled walls were all bare. But on the floor all around them, fifty- and hundred-dollar bills lay scattered like crisp, new confetti. The flat-screen TV propped against the far wall was enormous and new. Billie would get around to hanging it up eventually. The assault rifle leaning against the couch cost about as much as a new Mustang.

By now, the hound dog was barking. Billie's burner kept ringing. After sending three unanswered texts, Frank had taken to calling and calling and calling again.

Fully awakened by the third call, Billie jumped up from the couch.

"Mr. John," he said, using the name he knew Frank by.

Frank spoke briefly, and Billie replied.

"Okay, then," he said as he rubbed a bit of crust out of his sunken eye sockets. "Look, I am down for whatever. But listen here: If we're going to go 'head with this, you're going to *have* to pay the next install-ment. Then there's some other expenses that we'll talk about."

Billie Earl Johnson knew full well that in East Texas, $750,000 was not the going rate for *any* job — even when that job was the murder of a nice churchgoing lady like Nancy Howard.

But if that's what this man, Mr. John, was willing to pay, who was Billie to keep him from getting strung along and along? Especially when Billie was the one doing the stringing?

It had worked out so well for so long now that Billie and Stacey and all the folks they knew — even a few folks that Billie and Stacey didn't *like,* in particular — had been swimming, practically doing the backstroke, in Mr. John's money.

"Hell," he said as he snapped the cell phone shut. "At this rate, no one's even got to get killed."

Most likely, Billie thought, no one was *going* to get killed — and, like Stacey also thought, he had good reason to think so.

After all, Billie Earl Johnson and Mr. John had been having this same conversation, with only the slightest variations, for over a year.

■ ■ ■ ■

PART TWO:
NOVEMBER 2010

■ ■ ■ ■

CHAPTER 7

Billie

One year earlier — thirteen months to be exact — Frank Howard was taking his own sweet time trying on cowboy hats at Sheplers Western wear store in Mesquite, Texas.

Mesquite was an hour west of Ben Wheeler, and Frank had spent the time it would have taken to drive half that distance admiring himself in the mirror, twisting this way and that, pulling the hats low over his eyes, tipping them high up above his forehead. He had just about decided to buy a black, broad-brimmed, Stetson Bozeman hat when he saw Billie Earl Johnson standing a few yards away from him, watching.

Although Billie had been standing there for some time now, he didn't feel like he'd been looking at much.

Billie had spent a third of his forty-nine years behind bars. He knew a criminal when he met a criminal. But in Frank — or "Mr.

John" — Billie felt as though he'd made something more useful than another casual, criminal acquaintance.

He felt as if he'd made out an easy mark.

For months now, Billie had been taking Mr. John's money. Tens of thousands of dollars at a time — sometimes much more. The first time, it was $60,000 in cash. They'd been sitting in Mr. John's Lexus at the time. The money sat between them in a paper bag that also contained a photo of the woman Mr. John wanted killed.

On that occasion, Mr. John had told him to make the death look like an accident.

Billie had said, "Sure," adding only that "these things, done professionally, take some time."

What had happened after that was, basically, nothing — except insofar as Billie had turned himself into the big man in town, handing $100 bills out to all the folks he'd grown up with in Ben Wheeler. He'd bought motorcycles, four-wheelers, and a big four-door pickup for himself. He'd bought a Firebird for his daughter. He'd also bought thousands of dollars' worth of meth and shacked up with Stacey, partying and screwing for days on end. One day in town, the cops had picked him up for possession. But that was no big deal in the greater scheme of things. When he bonded out a few days later, he just called Mr. John and casually asked for more money.

The pattern had long since established itself, with Billie telling Mr. John he'd do the job, then coming up with some excuse or another that prevented him from doing the job. The one constant was that he'd always ask for more money.

The other constant was, he'd always get it.

Billie was surprised. He'd always been a good liar. A *great* liar, in fact. In some other life, he believed, he could have been one of the country's great con men. And his excuses were always believable because they were always close to the truth. If Billie had to tell Mr. John that he'd have to delay the job on account of illness, it was because he really had been sick. If the cause was that Billie had found himself behind bars and needed to be bonded out, it was because he really had gotten himself into trouble again.

And Billie was *always* getting into trouble.

But even so, there had been so *many* excuses, stretched over so many months. Sometimes, Billie felt as though Mr. John was paying him *not* to kill Nancy Howard. Or if he was paying to not kill her *just yet.*

Sometimes, Billie wondered if Mr. John

really did want this thing done. Sometimes he thought that the man was plain stupid. Stacey's own theory was that, like all the men she'd run across, Mr. John didn't know *what* he wanted. And what he'd been paying for was the luxury of not having to find out. In Stacey's estimation, *planning* to have Nancy Howard knocked off made Mr. John feel free. But on some level, Mr. John had to know that *doing* the thing would make him feel terrible.

As far as Stacey was concerned, Mr. John paid Billie to talk — to make his fantasy about life without Nancy feel more real — and paying more and more stretched the fantasy out, while making it feel that much more real.

Stacey's take on the situation sounded reasonable enough to Billie. As long as Mr. John kept paying, who was he to complain? And Mr. John *did* pay: twenty grand here, seventy there. Billie Earl burned through it all like a blowtorch through butter. As far as he even kept track, Billie figured he'd spent $750,000 or more just for coming up with a long line of excuses. Mr. John was not happy. He'd made that much clear. But for reasons that Billie could never quite fathom, that didn't keep Mr. John from paying him. So, here they were at Sheplers, and Billie was sure that Mr. John would have a fat envelope full of cash on his person.

"Everything's set," Billie said, after the two men had exchanged a perfunctory greeting.

"Everything?" said Mr. John.

"Everything except the next installment," said Billie. "I'm going to need that, if we're to proceed."

"Okay, then."

In the store's dressing room, Mr. John patted his pocket and took the envelope out.

"I want your assurance," he said. "I want your word this is going to happen."

Billie laughed as he grabbed the envelope out of Mr. John's hand.

"You've got it, partner," he said. "You've got it."

CHAPTER 8

Frank

Frank didn't like it one bit, this Billie Earl Johnson business he'd gotten involved with. His alter ego, "Mr. John," didn't sit comfortably with Frank, either.

The whole sordid scheme was a far cry from the good thing he had going with Suzanne.

But Frank knew that the plans he'd hatched with Billie Earl were the flip side of that good thing. Frank *could* have divorced Nancy, sure. He'd been divorced when he'd met her. But Frank's first marriage had not produced any children. He and his wife had been very young — that had made for an easy divorce. He was much older now, a pillar of the community, and a father. The children would make things especially hard. Frank's kids *knew* what a good man he was. He'd never want them to see him in the wrong kind of light. Compared to the harm that would do, life without Nancy would only be a small mercy.

Then there was the secondary consideration: Given a few things he'd been up to in secret over at his accounting practice — given the millions of dollars he'd stolen from his boss, Richard Raley — Frank simply could not *afford* to have some divorce court judge go through his financials with a fine-toothed comb. As far as Frank was concerned, filing for divorce was the same as walking into his local police station and turning himself in for embezzlement. And that was not something Frank Howard was willing to do.

So the question was, was Billie Earl Johnson the man for the job?

Sometimes it seemed to Frank that he'd been dealing with an imbecile. Already, on several occasions, he'd had to bond Billie Earl out of jail. But the thing he'd paid Billie for, time and again, never got done. Suzanne was on his back every day now about leaving Nancy, and he really had run out of excuses, while Billie Earl was full of them. Excuses poured out of the man like brown water pouring out of a broken Ben Wheeler faucet.

If Frank had known what all to do about it, he'd have done it. But it was too late now that he'd doubled down, again and again, with the money. He had to get something back for his investment.

And yet, Billie Earl got up the nerve to count his money — money he'd done nothing to earn yet — right in front of Frank's face.

"It's not the kind of job you rush, Johnny."

"I'm not telling you to rush it. I'm just saying it needs to happen soon. Sooner than soon, in fact."

"Why's that, Johnny? You gonna go to the Better Business Bureau? The Chamber of Commerce? Your local police? Come to think of it, maybe the police *would* like to learn more about you."

This was not a turn that Frank wanted his conversation with Billie Earl to take.

"Just do it," he snapped on his way out of the Western wear store. Seething now and seeing red, Frank was breathing quickly, shaking his head, more upset than he'd allowed himself to be with Billie Earl up to this point. So upset that he didn't see Billie Earl's girlfriend, Stacey, standing in the parking lot a few yards away with her cell phone held in front of her.

"What's that for?" Billie asked moments later, after John drove away, when she showed him the picture she'd snapped.

46

"Insurance," said Stacey. "Honestly, that man doesn't *know* what he's doing. He might be playing us two ways, for all we know."

"Nah," Billie said. "He may have money, but I still say that he's as dumb as a rock."

CHAPTER 9

Billie

Sometimes Billie wished that Mr. John could have gotten a glimpse of where all his money had gone.

The way he'd single-handedly propped up the local economy of Ben Wheeler, Texas.

The bartender at Billie's local biker bar had been one especially grateful recipient of Mr. John's generosity. And so, on Thanksgiving weekend, Billie; Stacey; Stacey's son, Dustin; and a whole host of East Texas knuckleheads gathered there, helping themselves to the bartender's endless supply of booze and ducking in and out of the bathrooms, where pills and powders were being bought and sold. Way in the back of the bar, in the shadows, an ex-con named Michael Lorence lit one match after another and flicked them into an empty beer bottle.

Dustin eyed Lorence suspiciously. The man was a stranger in a bar where everyone always knew everyone else. But Lorence did not make eye contact.

"Hey, partner," Dustin said.

The stranger did not respond. He kept his eyes on his matches, and Dustin let the matter drop.

When Dustin looked the stranger's way again, he saw that the man had gone, slipping quietly out of the bar.

The Firebird Billie had bought for his daughter was parked outside, though she wouldn't be driving it for a while. At least not until Billie paid to fix the windshield he'd smashed up with an old Louisville Slugger.

Billie's new bike was out there, too, but it was in even sorrier shape, since Billie, probably high on meth, had decided to drag the motorcycle around on a chain behind his new pickup truck.

Billie didn't know why he did these things. Long-term thinking and planning ahead had never been his strong suits. Meanness was what Billie brought to the family table.

"Boy," an uncle had said to him when he was young, "it's like you've got all this poison inside you. Deep down, like oil buried underground, eating away at your guts. Soon as something breaks through the surface, that oil's going to gush, and it's going to be black, and not you or no one else is going to have the wherewithal to control it."

Billie's uncle was wrong. Billie had all sorts of nasty stuff inside. But he also had perfect control. If he wanted to not bash up his bike, he wouldn't have done it. If he wanted to not bash in his daughter's windshield, he wouldn't have done that either. What the people around him did not understand was that Billie *wanted* to do all the things that he did. And age hadn't mellowed him out at all.

"Heya!" he shouted as his nephew Michael Speck walked into the bar. "Grab a stool. This round and every round's on Mr. John!"

Michael ordered a Jack on the rocks and a Michelob chaser. Scanning the room, he saw Stacey and Dustin hunched over at one of the banquettes.

"What's going on with that now anyways?"

"Same old," said Billie. "Dude's dumb as a goldfish but flush as a Saudi Arabian prince."

"And that thing he keeps talking about?"

"We'll talk about that, too, at some point," said Billie. "For now, let's have a toast!"

Over at their banquette, Stacey and Dustin perked up. The bartender hit Mute on the TV, poured himself a shot, and held the glass up as Billie raised his own glass and said, "Here's to the human ATM!"

"To Mr. Johnny!" the others joined in.

CHAPTER 10

Frank

Frank's bookkeeper had been working for him for years now. She went to First Baptist, as the Howards did, and once in a while Frank and Nancy would have her over for dinner. Frank knew her to be an honest woman, and extremely efficient and detail-oriented. Still, he was startled when she came into his office unannounced a few days after Thanksgiving weekend.

"Mr. Howard," she said. "I'm not sure about this. But it seems to me there's some sort of discrepancy?"

Looking up, Frank made a quick calculation: Should he switch his computer screen to hide the spreadsheet he'd been working on and thereby risk raising her suspicions? Should he leave the spreadsheet up and risk her catching a glimpse of the numbers he'd been moving around?

Turning toward her in his swivel chair,

Frank switched the screen off entirely.

"This company here —" the bookkeeper began, before Frank cut her off.

"That's the file I've been looking for!"

Frank grabbed the file, flipped it open, and glanced at the printout inside — paperwork relating to one of several holding corporations he'd set up to skim money from Richard Raley's company, American United Logistics. Raley's contracts with the Department of Defense were staggering. Frank couldn't *believe* how much ice Raley had shipped to the Middle East. He'd been even more surprised when he learned about the amounts that Raley had earned in return. At first, Frank had thought the sums involved wouldn't be missed. Also, he happened to know that Raley himself had a habit of going *off the rez.* There was a drug conviction in Raley's background. An arrest for drunk driving, which Raley had pleaded no contest to. How clued in could the businessman possibly be?

Still, the numbers involved were significant. And with Frank funneling more and more money off to Suzanne, and to Billie Earl Johnson, the amounts had gotten out of hand. Frank had stolen millions of dollars already. He intended to skim millions more. So, at this particular moment, the fact that his bookkeeper was good at her job was beginning to look like a terrible thing.

"Look at this, darlin'," Frank said. "You're absolutely right. The sums in this column don't add up."

Clearly, Frank had been making mistakes. Keeping track of the holding corporations, along with all of the attendant transactions, had been taking up more and more of his time. And given his business with Billie Earl Johnson, Frank Howard couldn't afford to draw attention to *any* of his secret dealings, especially now.

The thought of some dumbass, backwater divorce court judge poring over his financial dealings gave Frank the shivers. And now, sitting here with his bookkeeper's stack of folders, Frank felt a panic attack coming on. What looked like a windfall, when Richard Raley first appeared on his radar, was starting to feel more and more like a trap.

"Mr. Howard," the bookkeeper said. "Are you okay?"

"This is excellent work," he said after a moment. "Excellent, because this stuff's such a maze, such a headache. I'm impressed you found these errors. Why don't I take it home with me tonight to look it over and fix it up and put you onto this other account that's been troubling us?"

CHAPTER 11

Frank, Suzanne, and Nancy

That same weekend, Suzanne floated through her bedroom in Santa Cruz, gliding like a ghost across the thick, red carpet. She was dressed for a big night on the town. But Frank, lost in thought in front of his laptop at the edge of the bed, didn't notice her dress or her hair, or even the perfume she'd put on to please him.

Glasses halfway down his nose, he was lost in the same old spreadsheets, moving the same substantial number in and out of different columns, looking for a place to hide the millions of dollars he'd stolen in the elaborate shell game he'd been playing with Raley's money.

"Frank?" Suzanne said, softly at first. Then she said, *"Frank?"*

It was no use when he was like this. Lost in thought, quick to erupt in anger. There was a side to the man, it turned out, that

Suzanne hadn't expected to see.

Now that she had seen it, she didn't like it. But before she could say anything else, Frank's cell phone started to ring. Without a doubt, it was Nancy again with some kind of "crisis." With that woman it was always one thing or another.

This time, she was calling to tell Frank that the neighborhood kids had knocked over their mailbox. Did Nancy honestly think there was something Frank could do about that while he was away on "business"? There was nothing to do now but listen while Nancy talked and talked, moving from the mailbox to a litany of complaints about other things Frank couldn't fix from afar. The woman was lonely for him, Frank supposed. But there was nothing he could do about that either. Not when he wanted to be with Suzanne and couldn't stand his wife.

"Sorry, babe," Frank said in a whisper, cupping the phone in his hand. But Suzanne had already grown impatient. She whispered back, "End the call!"

"Nothing, sweetie," Frank said into the receiver. "That's just the TV in the background."

Now Suzanne was truly incensed.

"You're never going to leave her, are you!"

56

she said when Frank finally got off the phone. As far as Suzanne was concerned, Frank and Nancy had that much in common: With Frank, it was always one thing or another. If it wasn't work, it was Nancy's fibromyalgia. If it wasn't Nancy's illness, it was Ashley's graduation. It was always *something* with Frank, and for the first time, Suzanne was feeling close to the end of her rope.

"Maybe I should tell Nancy myself," she said. "Tell her what's going on with her loving husband. I bet your precious children would be thrilled to hear all about it."

"Baby," Frank told her. "What I'm sitting here doing is sorting things out. For you. For us. So that we can be together, truly."

Suzanne shrugged, even as part of her softened. She had to give Frank that much credit: The man could sweet-talk like nobody's business. But as she sat down on his lap, Frank suddenly started and jerked away from her. Maybe he'd put a hit out on the wrong woman after all.

That evening, after they'd gotten back from the restaurant, Frank turned on the shower, sat down on the toilet, and used his burner phone to call Billie Earl Johnson in Ben Wheeler, Texas.

"Man," he said, "you've got to get rid of

57

her. Yes, yes. I sent you a wire last week."

Frank paused for a moment. The bathroom had filled up with steam and he took his glasses off to wipe them down as he listened to what Billie Earl had to say.

"Aw, Jesus," he said when the hit man had finished. "Okay, okay. You'll have more by the end of the day. But I need your word, man, 'cause this has got to get done already."

■ ■ ■ ■

PART THREE:
JANUARY 2011

■ ■ ■ ■

CHAPTER 12

Billie

"Jesus," Mr. John was saying. "Okay, okay. You'll have more by the end of the day. But I need your word, man, 'cause this has got to get done already!"

Billie and Stacey had spent the morning getting as high as hot-air balloons and the afternoon flipping through brochures for a new four-door truck. At this late stage in Billie's long relationship with four-wheeled vehicles, it had become easier to just buy new ones than fix up the ones that he'd crashed — which was something that he did quite often, and with no small degree of satisfaction.

"You don't understand," he'd been saying to Stacey. "I didn't have an *accident.* I crashed that sucker on purpose; nothing accidental about it."

Then Mr. John had burst in with his phone call, interrupting the lecture that

Billie was about to give.

"Yes," Billie said, once the man had finally stopped his talking. "Yes, it's got to happen soon. And, for the hundredth time, yes — I got the address."

At first, Mr. John had wanted to make Nancy's death look like an accident. Billie would run her car off the road or push her off the balcony of the hotel rooms she booked for getaway weekends with friends from the church. But Billie had had his excuses for every occasion: He'd followed Nancy for days, but the perfect occasion had never presented itself.

He'd booked the hotel room next to Nancy's several times, only to find that, each time, Nancy would invite one of her friends to share the room.

Then there were Billie's medical excuses: seizures he suffered from. Dizzy spells. Blackouts. What it all led up to, Billie had said, was brain tumors.

Mr. John had swallowed all of those excuses — swallowed them down like syrup. But as time went by, his ideas about what to do with Nancy Howard got more fantastic, violent, and wild:

— Have her beaten to death with a base-

62

ball bat while scrapbooking with neighbors.

— Have her beaten to death with a tire
iron at her book club.

— Have her shot with an assault rifle while
having lunch with her church friends.
(To cover his tracks, Mr. John had told
him, Billie could spray the whole restaurant with gunfire.)

Christ, Billie had thought. *What did this
woman ever* do *to him?*

But here Billie was, swearing yet again that
he would take care of the whole sorry business.

If all went well, Mr. John told him in part-
ing, there might be another target in the
works. A job that would be even easier to
pull off and would pay even more.

CHAPTER 13

Suzanne

A few weeks later, a shabby old van pulled into the driveway at Suzanne's house in Santa Cruz. It was the rainy season in California's South Bay, drizzling for days now with no sign of stopping, and the rain muffled the sound of the van's rattling engine.

Suzanne wouldn't have heard the van anyway. She was lost in thought, as she had been ever since the rain had started. Cooped up indoors, she'd been running her love affair with Frank Howard over and over again in her head. She loved the man; that much was a given. But it was becoming increasingly clear she did not understand him. His moods and promises. The way he'd snap at her one moment, then want to make love the next. It had been a few weeks since she'd seen him and with each phone call he seemed to have grown more and more distant.

Out in the driveway the van's engine shut off. The door opened slowly. The man paused for a moment and leaned on the door.

In his left hand he held a cardboard box, about the length of a rifle.

Upstairs in her bedroom, Suzanne picked up the phone, then put it down again in its cradle. She needed to tell Frank that she needed him — here in California, where their future life would be. She felt that Nancy had lost him already. There were no reasons she could think of to drag things out.

She knew that she could be handling her love affair better. The guilt trips she'd taken to laying on Frank had all been counterproductive. She hoped that Frank knew she hadn't meant her threats. She would *never* tell Nancy about the affair. She just didn't know how else to push him. One way or another, Frank would have to pull the trigger on his divorce. All she'd been trying to do was help. But now she wondered if what she'd been doing had been pushing Frank further away.

She'd call him now and apologize for the way she'd been acting. If she *had* been pushing him, she'd take responsibility for it — own her actions while making Frank see how worn out she was from all this time spent apart from her lover.

"I love you, baby," she'd say, and tell him about the things she'd do to him the next time they met. But before she could do that, she heard the doorbell ringing downstairs.

"One moment!" she called out, and peeked out the window. The driver was there, rain drizzling off his baseball cap, holding the cardboard box, shifting his weight from one foot to the other.

Downstairs, she opened the door.

"From Mr. Frank Howard," the driver said.

"Yes?" said Suzanne.

The driver shifted his weight again, looked down at the ground, and back up at Suzanne. He seemed to be stoned or hungover, in which case it must have been a party for the ages.

"You'll have to sign here," the man said finally.

He took out a pocket-sized clipboard and handed Suzanne a pen.

Suzanne watched the van drive away, holding the cardboard box close to her chest. For a moment she had the strange sensation that something inside the package was ticking, but, no, it was only the beating of her own heart. Inside the house, she opened the box and read the card it contained:

"Babe," Frank had written. "You have to know I love you and that I'm doing everything I can as fast as I can to be with my California girl always."

It was just what Suzanne had been needing to hear. The fact that Frank had known it had to be proof that he really did love her. And, of course, the expensive bouquet of flowers that the box contained was beautiful.

CHAPTER 14

Nancy and Frank

Back in Carrollton, Texas, Nancy had finally talked Frank into going to therapy. From the get-go, she'd understood his resistance. Locally, the Howards had always been the family that others looked to for help. Admitting their own need for help did not come easily or naturally to them. But there was nothing easy or natural about the distance that had sprung up between them, either. Nancy had run out of ideas. And Frank would just glare and clam up when she brought up the state of their relationship.

Thankfully, their minister understood all of this and guided them with a firm, kindly hand as Nancy laid their problems out before him. Shy as she was, Nancy was also devoted. She'd told Frank so many times that she would do anything to heal this inexplicable rift in their marriage. Told him about how much she'd been looking forward to their years as empty nesters. About how good it would feel to rekindle the spark that had led to their marriage. She was sure that, together, they could fan love's flames higher than they'd ever been. But Nancy had also begun to understand that if she had any chance of pulling Frank back from the ledge, she'd have to make him see just how bad things had gotten.

"Frank," she said. "What we have here is a *crisis.*"

There on the couch in their minister's office, Frank felt like he was dying beside her.

The minister's face blurred. Nancy's words had all stopped making sense.

Only the word *divorce* snapped him back to attention.

Divorce was something Frank could not afford. Not in the eyes of his children. And not in the eyes of Nancy's lawyers — lawyers who'd charge $500 an hour to go through his finances and find Lord-knew-what when they got to his dealings with Richard Raley.

"No, honey," he said quickly. "Believe me, things are going to get so much better."

"Oh, Frank. I *want* to believe you. But I just don't know what to do."

Out in the parking lot of their church, Nancy said goodbye, tearfully.

"Do you want a ride home?" Frank asked.

"I'll walk home, sweetie. To clear my head."

But Nancy's head was still cloudy as she crossed the road in front of the church.

Out of nowhere, a four-door pickup appeared. Moving much too fast, it nearly knocked her into the gutter.

Instinctively, Nancy's head flew up to clutch the cross around her neck.

"That was a close one," she gasped. But there was no one there to hear her.

CHAPTER 15

Billie

It was Billie's idea to have this meeting today. He wasn't far from Carrollton, anyway, killing time at Bass Pro Shops, a cavernous hunting and fishing store outside of Dallas.

With its in-house shooting gallery, archery range, and brewpub, BPS could almost be an amusement park, and Billie had been looking forward to getting some quality R&R in — trying a few rifles out, maybe a crossbow. Stacey had come along for the ride and had invited her son, Dustin, and Billie's nephew, Michael, to go with them to meet Mr. John.

Billie had mixed feelings about these youngsters he had in tow.

Up to this point, he'd been happy to spread Mr. John's money around. But Billie'd been stringing Mr. John along for so long now, sooner or later the well was bound to run dry. Billie'd burned through so much of the money already that he was starting to feel like he really ought to be looking out for himself at this point.

On the other hand, Billie knew that he'd begun to run out of excuses, so if Mr. John *did* threaten to call it quits, he could always shift the blame over to Dustin and Speck.

All in all, it might not be the worst thing to have them along. And as things turned out, Speck was the one who ended up doing most of the talking while Billie nursed his beer.

By the end of the meeting, he'd hatched a whole new plot with Mr. John.

What it amounted to was this: Nancy Howard had been planning a trip to San Marcos — the Texas town where she and Frank Howard had first met. Speck would follow her, shoot her there, and take a cellphone photograph of her corpse, which he would show to Mr. John in person back up in Carrollton.

Once he'd seen it, Mr. John would give Billie, Stacey, Dustin, and Speck $100,000, drawn on Nancy's life insurance policy, which they would split between them.

Then he'd pay them $5,000 a week — money that they would split too — for the rest of their lives.

Billie did the math in his head: That was a quarter million dollars a year, give or take. And if Mr. John changed his mind about paying, Stacey had enough dirt on the man to blackmail him into paying whatever he had left. Either way, they were going to get their hands on every last cent of Mr. John's money.

For the first time, the thought of actually *killing* Nancy Howard — instead of just stringing Mr. John along, and along, and along — seemed like the best way to go.

CHAPTER 16

Frank and Dustin

Frank was in his Lexus, listening to Christian radio, driving toward Ben Wheeler to talk to Dustin in person.

"For out of the heart proceed evil thoughts," the radio minster was saying, *"murders, adulteries, fornications . . ."*

Dustin had been calling Frank pretty much nightly. But for a few nights now, he hadn't been making a whole lot of sense.

What Frank knew already was that Billie and Stacey had ended up behind bars, yet again. What Frank did *not* understand was what their latest arrest had to do with the fact that Nancy had already been down to San Marcos and managed to get herself back in one piece.

"The evil deeds of the wicked ensnare them; the cords of their sins hold them fast . . ."

Frank turned the radio off in disgust. On the floor under his feet was a bag full of

74

money — big bills, packed tightly and bound with blue elastic bands. Frank tossed the bag in the backseat as he pulled up the driveway. He saw the Firebird with its bashed-in windshield, the lawn full of weeds, the screen door hanging off one of its hinges.

"It's *one* way to live," Frank mumbled to himself under his breath.

"My mom," Dustin said to him once he came inside. "She's not doing too well in there, in County."

"I wouldn't expect that she would be," said Frank.

He looked around the room. Dustin was nineteen. Old enough to get by on his own. But he'd been living with Michael Speck for a few weeks now, ever since Billie and Stacey's arrest. From what Frank could see, this domestic arrangement was not working out for the kid. Speck was nowhere to be seen, and Dustin looked like he was barely there. His face was unnaturally pale, except for the deep, purple bags under his eyes. He was wild-eyed and smelled almost moldy, like an old shower curtain. When Dustin spoke, his words ran into each other.

"You really want to help your momma?" Frank said.

Earnestly, Dustin said, "I would do any-thing."

"Iwoodoo *any*thang" was what it sounded like.

"The best thing to do," Frank told him, "is the job you all signed up for."

"*Any*thang," Dustin said.

Frank walked back out to the Lexus and returned a moment later, carrying a crumpled-up paper bag.

"Here," he told Dustin. "Take this and use it to bail your mom out of jail. Then go and buy yourself a baseball bat. Wait for my call. And then drive out to Gaylord. You know where Gaylord is? In Grapevine, less than an hour outside of Dallas. Nancy's go-ing to a convention there. I'll give you the name of the hotel she's at. You'll sneak in and use your baseball bat on her. Use it real good. And make sure to get pictures."

"Thank you," Dustin said. "Mr. John, you can be sure we'll take care of this for you."

"And, Dustin? There's just one more thing. This business in San Marcos didn't work out for us. So I've been thinking, we should have a contingency plan. This con-vention that Nancy's going to, it won't be for a while now. Why don't you drive up to Carrollton in the meantime. See the lay of the land. I'm sure there's a good way to do it there too. Maybe a burglary. Maybe a fire."

Dustin did not know what *contingency* meant. But everything else Mr. John said made good sense to him.

"Sure," he said. "Fire sounds like a real good way to go."

■ ■ ■ ■

PART FOUR:
JULY 2012

■ ■ ■ ■

CHAPTER 17

Dustin

It was nighttime in Carrollton, and Dustin was driving a rented Honda Accord around and around and *around* the whole town, high on the methamphetamine he'd been smoking, every waking minute of every day, ever since he'd moved in with Michael Speck.

It had been a few weeks now since Mr. John had driven out to talk to him about bailing his mom out of jail. The money that Mr. John left behind totaled $24,000. And the first thing that Dustin had done was go out and buy himself the biggest bag of methamphetamine anyone in Ben Wheeler had ever seen. He'd smoked a lot of that crank himself, and shared freely with friends and neighbors.

After a few sleepless nights, he'd taken to posting selfies on Facebook — stacks of hundred-dollar bills all around.

A few nights after that, when eight thousand dollars blew off the hood of his car, he didn't even bother to scoop the money back up.

Then, with the money all gone, Dustin had called Mr. John and done what he'd seen Billie do countless times. Just like that, he asked for more money. And, just like that, Mr. John had agreed. The convention in Gaylord was still a few weeks away. But Dustin was more than willing to drive up to Carrollton.

"Okay," Mr. John had told him. "I'll hide some cash for you up here. You can drive up and pick it up. But you know what you'll have to do here to earn it."

The streets in Carrollton didn't make any sense to Dustin. The houses all looked like the same great big house, and he couldn't make heads or tails of the neighborhoods.

"Frankford Estates," he mumbled to himself in the front seat. "Parkside Estates. What's up with this town anyway?"

There was a can of gasoline in the trunk and a box of bullets in Dustin's lap. But the box had spilled over, and now there were bullets all over his lap, on the seat under him, and on the floor, rolling this way and that in the Honda. There was also a map, which Dustin had given up on, and a slip of paper, on which he'd written the address that Mr. John had given him. Dustin must have been high when he'd written it down — he could not make sense of it *at all*. And so he drove, around and around for hours in circles, in squares, and in zigzags, without getting closer to where it was that he needed to be.

It was as if he were driving underwater.

Exasperated, he pulled the car over. There, in the driver's seat, he'd gripped the wheel with both hands, closed his eyes tightly, and breathed, in and out, until the white noise in his head died down to a whisper. He checked the address once again — this time, he could almost make out words and numbers. He took out the gun he'd brought — a silver .380 that Speck had lent him — and checked it too.

Having centered himself, he put the car key back in the ignition, turned the engine on, pulled out into the night — and promptly got lost. He turned the rental car around, and then around again. He made one wrong turn, then made another. Then, giving up on the whole enterprise, he made one final U-turn.

As he did so, the Honda's headlights swept across a driveway. And there, standing outside, he saw Nancy Howard.

CHAPTER 18

Bethany Wright

Dustin recognized her right away — recognized her from one of the photos that Mr. John had shown him. Except now she was wearing a nightgown, slippers, and a bathrobe. Nancy looked lost in thought, walking a recycling bin down to the end of her driveway.

Dustin could not believe his luck. Quickly, he turned off his headlights, ducked down in the driver's seat, counted to twenty. When he came back up in his seat, Nancy Howard was gone. But he knew which house was hers now, and he was ready.

Quietly, he gathered the bullets off his lap and the seat and the floor. He made sure his gun was loaded. He closed his eyes yet again. It had been a few hours now since his last hit, and though his head was still cloudy he was grateful for it — the drug would help him do what he couldn't do sober.

"I'll count to two hundred," he told himself. "Give her a few minutes to get in bed."

He'd counted to sixty when the police siren sounded behind him.

Officer Bethany Wright had had her eye on Dustin for some time, seen him circling the neighborhoods, pulling over at random, then starting again. He'd been driving so slowly, the cop hadn't had much of a reason to stop him. But now that Dustin was just sitting there, in his car, with the headlights off and his engine still on, Wright felt that she had sufficient reason to question him.

"Sir," she said as walked up to the driver's side door and looked at the kid inside, pale and jittery in his threadbare Batman T-shirt. "How long have you been in Carrollton tonight?"

Dustin was breathing heavily. He'd had just enough time to hide the gun under the passenger seat.

"Been trying to find my uncle's house now for two, three, four hours," he said with a long, heavy sigh.

"The reason I ask is, I saw you earlier. And now I see you again . . ."

"Yeah. I was going in circles. Circles and

85

circles. Circles and circles and circles and circles . . ."

Officer Wright fingered the strap on her holster. What the computer in her squad car had told her was that the Honda was a hundred miles away from its point of origin. And, even if the car was in the right place, the man sitting behind the wheel belonged elsewhere. Carrollton was an upscale town, easy and quiet. Sometimes the local kids would smoke grass or get drunk and dumb out in their pickups. But this kid, who could not have been older than twenty, was strung out on meth. That much was clear: He had that moldy shower-curtain smell that truly committed meth heads would get on their binges. And when the officer asked for his license — the kid was nineteen, it turned out — she saw that he was from a methed-out town in East Texas and didn't belong in Carrollton at all.

"Will you please step out of the car?" she asked.

CHAPTER 19

Dustin

Dustin was dazed, but not too dazed to know that he had not broken the law just yet.

He stepped out quietly, calmly.

He thought he could talk his way out.

First, he told the lady cop that he'd come to Carrollton to borrow some money from his uncle.

A few seconds later, he said that he'd been looking for his stepfather.

A few seconds after that, he volunteered the information that his stepfather was in jail.

The lady cop didn't look fazed at all. But Dustin felt that his words were all coming out wrong, in a tangle that didn't convey how innocent his actions, up to that point, had been.

"Tell me again who you're visiting here," the cop instructed. " 'Cause now I'm confused. First you said 'uncle' and then you said —"

"His name's John," Dustin interrupted. "Okay? We always called him 'John.' That was it."

This was much better. So close to the truth, Dustin reasoned, it didn't even sound much like a lie.

It was just like Billie had told him: "Always stick close to the truth when you lie. So close that *you* believe everything you're saying."

Now Dustin was doing just that, and it didn't surprise him at all to see the cop smiling, or to feel himself smiling as well.

"Okay," she said. "So, John's . . . a friend of the family?"

"Yes. Basically."

"And what is your business with John?"

This was a curveball. But so far, the truth had seemed like a good strategy, and Dustin decided that he'd go all in.

"Okay," he said. "I'm not trying to cause no problems, ma'am. But the thing is I am a hit man. Like, a contract killer? I'm a hit man, and I'm up here in Carrollton —"

Even before he'd gotten the words out, it dawned on Dustin he'd made a mistake. A weird mistake, and it was weird, too, that although he'd commanded his mouth to stop talking, it kept on talking on its own accord.

"I'm up here to commit a hit," the mouth said. "A hit on a woman in Carrollton."

CHAPTER 20

Bethany Wright

Officer Wright had never met an honest to
goodness hit man. But you didn't need to
be Columbo or Kojak — anyone with op-
posable thumbs could see that Dustin was
too high to know what he was saying. For
all he seemed to know, he was at home playing video games.

Still, you could not have a kid like this
driving around town. Not in the shape he
was in.

Even in the back of her Carrollton PD
patrol car, the kid kept on talking, without
making much sense at all.

"Sir," the officer said. "I would seriously
advise you to zip it until we get down to the
station."

"Yes, ma'am," said Dustin, and for the
few minutes it took to get down to the station he actually managed to keep his mouth
shut. Inside, he was fingerprinted, photo-

graphed, and placed in a holding cell, where he sat, fidgeting on the hard cot, mumbling to himself.

"If they had me on murder, they'd send me to prison for certain," he said. "But I didn't *commit* any murder. The most they could get me on now is attempted murder. But how would the prove it? I told the lady cop I was a hit man. But it's not like she found my gun. And how could she know who I've killed, when I haven't killed *anybody* just yet?"

He was still mumbling when the officer finished up her arrest report. Dustin had been driving erratically. He was certainly under the influence of something, even though he wasn't drunk. The best thing to do, she thought, was hold him overnight, wait for him to sober up, and send him back to East Texas. She hoped the kid could get clean. While he was young. While it still made a difference. If he didn't, the cops in East Texas would put him away for something more meaningful than a traffic stop. And maybe that would be for the best. A kid so turned around that he couldn't tell the difference between video games and real life? Who thought he was an actual *hit man*?

Officer Wright had a certain amount of sympathy. She had teenage boys of her own.

And she knew how rough towns in East Texas could be. She also knew that what she could get on him now wouldn't lead to much more than a few days in County. And frankly, if Texas cops started locking up all the meth heads in Texas, the state's prisons would burst at the seams and a horde of *real* criminals would descend like some biblical plague.

Better to roll the dice on Dustin. Let the chips fall wherever they may — as long as they did not fall in Carrollton.

"Son," she said at the end of her shift early the next morning, after having filed her report, "now that you've slept it off, I'm going to ask you to get yourself right out of Carrollton. Whoever this John is, I don't see that finding him's going to do you much good. What you need, if you ask me, is a shower, a strong cup of coffee, and a long, hard look in the mirror. Is this really where you want to end up?"

Dustin rubbed his eyes. For the first time since his encounter with the lady cop, words failed him entirely. He gaped at her for a moment.

"Really?" he said. "Just like that?"

"Just this time," the officer said as she opened the holding cell door. "Just this once. And never again in this town, son."

CHAPTER 21

The Howards

A few weeks after Dustin's arrest in Carrollton, Frank and Nancy sat down to a romantic dinner at their home in Carrollton.

Nancy had looked forward to this meal for days now, planning this date night for over a week.

She'd shopped all day, soaked the beans the previous evening, had the beef on a slow boil since that afternoon. And if the tortillas were store bought, the guacamole and salsas were homemade and spicy, though not *too* spicy — just the way Frank had always liked them. Nancy had ironed the tablecloth to within an inch of its life. The linen napkins, which had thin, red lines around their borders, were the same ones she used when company came over. But tonight it would be just the two of them, eating and laughing together like newlyweds.

Nancy appreciated how sweet Frank had been when he'd come home from work that evening. He'd bought fancy chocolate, red roses — the works. He'd dimmed the lights when he walked into the dining room and told her how beautiful she looked.

He'd even asked her if she wasn't too cold, and although Frank loved to walk into cold rooms on hot summer nights, he'd turned the air conditioner down just a notch for her.

"That's the dress I bought you, honey?" he asked.

The expensive dress fit Nancy well — it even flattered her figure. She could tell Frank had picked it with care.

"Love you, honey bunny," she told him.

They were midway through the first course when Frank's phone buzzed. A few months ago, he would have picked it up, left the room — left the house, even. Raley, the defense contractor, seemed to have Frank coming and going at all hours, sometimes for days at a time.

But Frank seemed to know how special this evening was.

"Let it ring," he told Nancy, and reached out to take her hand.

"I want you to know how much I love

you," Frank said. "How much I appreciate everything you've done, and all that you're doing in this marriage."

"You make my life so rich," said Nancy.

The thing was, she meant it, even though it so awkward to say. The words weren't hers. Like Frank's, they were plucked from a list of affirmative sentences the minister had provided them with during one of their therapy sessions. But, Nancy thought, that didn't make them untrue.

Was it such a bad thing, working from a script that seemed to sum up so much of what they'd told him they felt for each other?

Nancy the homemaker. Frank the accountant.

Did that mean there was no room for poetry in their lives?

"Nancy," Frank said. "I just hope you know how much I value —"

Before he could finish, his phone buzzed again. This time, he took it out of his pocket.

"Shit," he said. "Shit, honey. I've *got* to get this."

Then she was alone at the table, watching the food that she'd made with such care grow cold as Frank talked and talked — the conversation seemed to go on forever — in the other room.

CHAPTER 22

Frank

"Jesus Christ," Frank said to Billie, while Nancy sat alone at the dinner table.

This was not how he wanted his very last evening with Nancy to go.

"This must be the third time you've called me for bail just *this year.*"

"You *promised,* Frank," said Billie. "You promised to bail me out. You said you'd post bail for Stacey. But here we are, sitting in lockup, not doing the one job you hired us for."

"The money's gone, Billie. And there's not going to *be* any more money for jobs that never get done."

It had been years now. *Years* of hearing the same old shit from Billie Earl Johnson. Years of putting up with him and Stacey — with Stacey's knuckleheaded son, Dustin, and with Billie's idiot nephew, Michael.

Years of this shit, and hundreds of thousands of dollars flushed down the drain in the past twelve months alone.

"The thing is, Frank, we've got a sure-fire plan. A plan that doesn't allow for mistakes. But that plan cannot be executed from here."

"I gave the last of the money to Michael."

"And that's money that Michael's earned, because he's the one who came up with this plan. But it's like I'm telling you: the plan only works if you post bail."

Nancy was moving around; Frank could hear it. Had she been eavesdropping on him? Or was all his skulking around turning him paranoid?

"Honey?" he hollered, poking his head out the door.

Nancy's not there, after all.

"Just getting some water, Frank!" she called back from the kitchen. But Frank's jittery now. Best to get off the line as soon as possible. This was why he hated it when Billie's calls caught him at home.

"And if I don't?" he said quietly into the receiver.

"*If* you don't, Frank, I'm looking at a corrections officer right now who would be *very* interested in certain stories that I could tell him. Stories about a woman in Carrollton. A mighty nice lady. Church lady, in fact.

97

And I could tell him at least a few things about the man this church lady lives with."

"Is that a threat, Billie?"

Frank's trying his best to sound hard while talking softly. Quiet menace was the tone he was going for.

"Are you *threatening* me?"

"What I'm *telling* you, Frank, is what things look like, to me, from the place where I'm sitting."

Frank poked his head out the door once again, put the phone down on his desk, and walked to the window. The Japanese maple outside his home office swayed gently in the August breeze. The neighbor's dog barked at the little girl who lived next door. The girl was bouncing up and down on her new trampoline, and Frank thought about his own children, about Suzanne and her girls, about Nancy. And now Billie Earl's ruined his last night with the woman.

"I'll send it," Frank said under his breath. He was about to say it into the receiver, but when he picked his cell phone back up, no one was there. Just a few moments ago, he was prepared to hang up on Billie.

Instead, Billie hung up on him.

It seemed like an hour had gone by. But checking his watch, Frank saw it'd been just a few minutes. He peeked into the dining room only to find Nancy waiting, patiently, hopefully, with her hands in her lap and the linen napkin stained, ever so slightly, with her mascara.

Crying again, Frank thought. He knew he'd been rude, getting up from the table, leaving Nancy alone as the dinner she made for them grew cold. But if he was going to be perfectly honest, he wasn't sure that he cared. Sometimes, he thought, it was as if Nancy simply didn't notice how hard he worked for this family of theirs. And even without Suzanne in the picture, he didn't see how he could keep on living with the woman. She'd been beautiful once. She had worshipped him. But when he looked at her now, Frank could barely see the beauty that he had fallen in love with. And instead of admiring him, all that Nancy seemed to do now was nag.

Who *was* this woman who'd taken the place of the Nancy he'd married?

She'd be dead anyway inside of a week. And so what if she didn't deserve what was coming her way? What did *deserving* mean anyway? Did Richard Raley deserve the millions he'd made off the government — made by shipping *ice* to a *desert*? Why did Raley deserve that money any more than Frank Howard did? He was a man who had spent his whole life taking care of Nancy, the kids, and their needs. But now, with the kids grown, hadn't the time come for Frank to look out for himself and his own happiness?

If Frank could have divorced Nancy, he would have. But the time for that was years earlier, before he'd started siphoning money out of Richard Raley's company. Frank couldn't risk being found out. And he certainly couldn't stomach the thought of spending another month — much less the rest of his life — with Nancy.

Frank could admit to himself now that he'd let Billie Earl Johnson get away with every excuse because, in his heart, he had hoped for a better solution. But years had gone by, with no other solutions presenting themselves. Life with Nancy was a lie — a lie that felt worse than death. And if someone had to die, why should it be Frank Howard?

Frank was a preacher's kid, not a killer. But ever since meeting Suzanne, he'd felt trapped — cornered like an animal — each time he'd come home to Carrollton and Nancy.

Everyone knew that cornered animals were not responsible for their actions. And that was the conclusion Frank had come to

when he became aware of Nancy, still crying in the next room.

It made Frank resentful, the fact that he'd
have to ask her forgiveness for taking the
call, that he'd have to pretend to kiss and
make up — that he'd have to spend one
more night with the woman he wanted dead.

CHAPTER 23

Frank and Nancy

But the next day, Frank had to admit the therapy was working — up to a point. Not enough to save his marriage. Not enough to make him love Nancy again. But enough to make him feel guilty about everything that was about to happen to her. That's what had upset him so much about last night's phone call. Frank had wanted to end things with Nancy on a high note. Instead, because of Billie's interruption, he'd had to deal with Nancy's tears. Tears at the table, and tears when he told her that he'd have to go away, the very next day, for work.

Frank's flight wasn't due to take off for a few hours more, and in the meantime, he was willing to play the part of a dutiful husband for a few more hours. All morning, Frank had been helping Nancy with the gift baskets she'd bring to church the next day for a ladies' lunch. Frank knew how much

Nancy looked forward to seeing her friends there. She would often take comfort in their companionship during his absences, which had grown more and more frequent.

The least Frank could do was help out one last time.

When he was done loading the minivan, Nancy leaned in for a hug. She kissed him on the lips, whispered, "I love you" in his ear.

Outside, it was raining. A break in the sweltering heat. And for a moment, Frank wondered if this trip was a mistake.

What if he *did* just end his affair with his California mistress, Suzanne?

If he did, what would Suzanne tell her daughters? What would happen to all the plans they had made? And had Suzanne seen the countless spreadsheets he'd been tweaking, hunched over his laptop, night after night, on nights they could have been gambling, or traveling together, or making love?

Did Suzanne have her suspicions? Frank didn't know. But he had suspicions of his own. He knew that Suzanne wasn't above making threats. And where there were threats, there was sometimes a fire, and could Frank really afford to take the risk? Especially now, when Billie had finally come up with a plan that was good?

Frank didn't know what the plan was, specifically. He'd told Billie he did not *want* to know. "Plausible deniability" — a phrase he'd heard once in a movie — seemed like the safest way. That's why he'd booked a ticket to California and told Nancy that he had to fly to Tampa for work. That's why he was leaving Carrollton today.

Frank did not *want* to know. Especially because he'd heard something different in Billie's voice in the course of their last conversation: The resolve it would take to actually end Nancy's life. Billie Earl Johnson was a criminal, sure. But even for a criminal, murder would be no small thing.

It was no wonder it had taken Billie so long to work up the nerve.

But now that the moment was here, Frank looked at Nancy and felt tender — affectionate, almost. How innocent she was, in regards to what would soon befall her. How she *looked* at him, even now, as her life drew to its close. That look made Frank feel powerful — and why not? After all, he truly was in control and the power he'd wield, through the instrument of Billie Earl Johnson, was almost godlike.

Hadn't Nancy promised him, years ago, to love him till death do they part?

Now she'd make good on that promise.

Standing out there in their driveway, Frank told her he'd only be gone for a couple of days. That all his traveling would wind down soon — he just knew it. When he got back this time, he'd take Nancy on a trip of their own. The romantic getaway they'd been talking about. Maybe they'd go snorkeling in St. John.

Maybe South America.

When they got home, they would have Brianna's wedding to look forward to. And after that, who knew, maybe grandkids?

"Lord willing!" said Nancy.

She told Frank to travel safely. She said that she'd be there, waiting for him, as soon as he found his way home.

CHAPTER 24

Nancy

Nancy was almost done with her lunch when Frank called the next day to check in.

Lunch was more of a tea, she told him. A tea that went late, and they never did eat, and it was getting to be seven thirty! The rain was still coming down, she said — harder now. But she was going to drop by Taco Bueno on her way home, get some takeout to eat while watching television.

If there's one good thing about all of Frank's traveling, it's that she gets to catch up on all of her shows.

As she drove, Nancy thought about how right she'd been to get Frank into marriage counseling. Lord knew he hadn't wanted to go. But now — especially now, with Frank agreeing to cut back on his traveling — she really could see what a fresh start would mean for them both.

At Taco Bueno, the girl behind the counter

screwed up Nancy's order — twice. Tried to give her a can of Coke instead of the sweet tea she'd ordered. A side of salsa and chips instead of guacamole. Nancy didn't care. She was smiling, still thinking of Frank. She was thinking of how good he'd been when he saw how upset she had gotten over the phone call he'd taken right in the middle of dinner. How sweet the make-up kiss he'd given her had been. Frank really was paying attention to her now, after so many months of seeming far away.

Nancy tipped the girl generously. Back in the car, she turned the radio on and sang along to the Christian rock station.

Six days. That's how long Frank's trip to Tampa was going to take. Six days of meetings. Six days she'd be lonely. But she had almost a week now to research vacation spots for them. St. John was Frank's idea. He always did love the water. Nancy had already been to South America. But that trip had been a mission for her church, and South America was so big, and so beautiful.

Maybe they could split the difference — fly down to the Virgin Islands for a week, then spend another week in Buenos Aires. Nancy would call the travel agent, work out flights and prices, before Frank got back. She'd surprise him, too, with the new calico curtains she'd had made for their bedroom and with the carpet swatches she had picked out for the den.

It was a lot to think about. A lot to juggle. But thinking about it made Nancy happy. It distracted her from thinking about how lonely she got when Frank wasn't around. And, as she drove, Nancy was so distracted that she did not notice the car that had been following her in the rain, tracking her from the church parking lot, down to the Taco Bueno, and all the way home, where that car sits now, engine idling, just outside Nancy's driveway while she pulls into her garage.

■ ■ ■ ■

PART FIVE:
AUGUST 2012

■ ■ ■ ■

CHAPTER 25

The Shooting of Nancy Howard

In the garage, Nancy shut the engine off, turned around, and grabbed the takeout bag from Taco Bueno from the backseat. She'd gotten her favorites — the Tex-Mex bowl, an order of cheesecake chimichangas to eat for dessert, and that supersized sweet tea. It's Saturday night, after all. Frank's in Tampa, and there's time to get three whole episodes of *Law & Order* in before going to bed.

She checked her text messages. Nothing from Frank. Nothing from her daughters. Nothing to break her reverie as she put the phone back in her purse.

Lost in her thoughts, she didn't see the man walking ever so slowly up her driveway, watching her, waiting for her to step out of the car as the rain fell around his feet, muffling the sound of his footsteps.

When she did get out of her car — purse

111

on her shoulder, takeout bag in hand — she had her back to the man. All that she heard was the sound of the rain.

But before Nancy could get to the door, she sensed that someone had come up behind her.

First, she felt his breath, hot on the back of her neck. Then she felt the man's arm, wrapping around her neck in a smooth, snakelike motion. The arm's thick and muscular. It pulled her backward, almost yanking her off her feet. And then, before she could think, she felt something cold, round, and hard pressing into the side of her head.

"Gimme your purse," said the man.

It's so sudden, this physical intrusion, Nancy didn't know *what* was happening. For a moment, she wondered if Frank had come home early. If this was all some sort of practical joke. Her heart was racing but everything else had slowed down, and she could feel her own blood as it pumped through her temples.

No. This man with his thick, snakelike arm wasn't Frank. Nancy knew Frank's smell. Knew Frank's voice. Nancy did not have to turn around to know that it was not her husband standing behind her.

For a moment they stand there, two silhouettes in a shadow cast by the open garage door. Then, without thinking, Nancy wrestles free of the man, spins on one heel, and stands there — face to face with a stranger.

"I said give me your purse," the man says again.

He's not young nor especially old — in his twenties or thirties — white, with brown hair and blue eyes under a black baseball hat.

As if in a daze, Nancy hands him the Taco Bueno takeout bag.

"Bitch, what are you *doing*?" says the man, letting the takeout bag fall to the ground. "Give me that damn *purse.*"

Still in her daze, Nancy slips the purse off her shoulder. But instead of handing it to him, she grabs the purse with both hands and surprises herself by shoving it, hard, toward the man's chest.

The violence of that unexpected shove startles Nancy, confusing her further. But the man doesn't look startled at all. The flash of anger Nancy had seen when she handed the man her takeout bag seems to have passed.

Now the man simply looks cold, and determined.

That expression does not change as he raises the gun and points it at Nancy's forehead, just above her left eye.

"Jesus!" she pleads. It's the first word she's spoken. "Save me!"

Then, as if in slow motion, she watches the man pull the trigger.

CHAPTER 26

Frank

The craps dealer looked up at Frank, who'd been on an incredible streak, rolling six sevens in a row. But Frank was looking down at his watch, adjusting for time zones, doing the math in his head.

It's eight in Dallas, where the clocks were two hours ahead. That made it nine o'clock in Florida.

Time to call Nancy.

"I'll be right back, babe," he said to Suzanne, excusing himself from the table.

"You okay, darling?"

"I just need some air."

It's a perfect evening in Tahoe. Seventy degrees out, dry as a bone, a slight breeze coming up from the water. Frank had a habit of checking the weather before calling home, just in case Nancy asked what the weather was like wherever it was she thought Frank was. Now his iPhone told him that it's as hot as a furnace in Tampa.

He fiddled with the phone some more, paced back and forth on the patio outside the casino.

There was a part of Frank that was afraid Nancy would pick up the phone when he called.

Another part of him knew that she wouldn't.

And when Frank finally *did* call his home, the phone rang and rang, then went to voice mail.

When he called Nancy's cell phone, it did the same thing.

Frank did not leave a message.

Suzanne was waiting for him inside the casino. His new life was waiting there with her. But only if Billie had actually made good on his promise. Billie, and whoever else Billie had picked for the job.

If there was one thing Frank knew, it was that Billie Earl and his associates had it in them to screw up.

Frank decided to wait a few minutes, then tried Nancy again.

His call went straight to her voice mail again. The same chirpy message, and this time, Frank left a message, making sure to sound a little concerned.

"Babe, I don't know where you are. But

116

I'm just finishing up for the day. These weekend meetings, I don't know why the company bothers. But I'll be home in a few days, and I'll call you tomorrow. And, Nancy, I love you and miss you."

For a moment, he almost believed what he was saying.

Then that moment passed. Gradually, the look of concern on Frank's face began to twist into a smile.

By the time he got back to the craps table where Suzanne was waiting, Frank was grinning from ear to ear.

CHAPTER 27

Nancy

A few minutes earlier, conscious but covered in blood, Nancy had crawled through her house, praying and pleading with Jesus and leaving a thick, red, bloody trail in her wake as she made her way into the bathroom, pushed herself up against the sink, steadied herself, and looked in the mirror.

She did not understand what she saw there. For a moment, she did not recognize her own face or remember how she had gotten into the bathroom.

Then she did remember. She remembered hearing God's voice: "Get up!" He had told her.

She remembered getting up.

Nancy remembered punching the OnStar button in her car, again and again, before she realized that her keys were gone and that without her car keys OnStar wouldn't work. She remembered punching the security code in on her burglar alarm to shut it off — something that had seemed so sensible when she'd done it but seemed ridiculous now, when she was desperate for help to come.

She should have let the alarm go off. Now she'd have to get to her kitchen and call 911 on the landline.

Steadying herself against the walls of her house, smearing them with more blood as she made her way, she finally reached the kitchen. And in the time that it took the 911 dispatcher to answer — time that was no time at all — Nancy recalled even more. She remembered the man with the gun. The determined look in his eyes. The few, simple things he had said. And the blazing pain that had preceded the darkness. Nancy remembered lying on the concrete floor of her garage. She recalled everything that had led up to the moment in which her Savior had told her to wake up. To get up. To *live.*

Now it was Nancy's turn to talk, to tell the 911 dispatcher what had happened, to ask for an ambulance and hold on until help arrived. As she dialed, she prayed for the strength it would take her to do it.

"Carrollton 911, what's the emergency?"

"I've been shot!" was all she could say in response.

Nancy's tongue felt fat and swollen. There was so much blood in her mouth, she could barely get the words out.

"Please," she said. "Oh God, oh God."

"What's the address, ma'am?"

Upset as Nancy was, it gave her strength to hear the dispatcher's calm voice.

"Breathe," she told herself. "Breathe and try again."

Slurring badly, she managed to give her address: "Forty-Five Bluebonnet Way."

"Tell me exactly what happened," the dispatcher said. But she could barely make out Nancy's answer: something about her garage. Being attacked *in* her garage?

Nancy was slurring so badly now the dispatcher couldn't be sure. Then, much more clearly, she said: "Please help me."

"Yes, ma'am," the dispatcher told her — help was already speeding toward Nancy. The trick now was to keep her conscious and talking until help arrived.

"Just stay on the line, ma'am, and I'm going to get some questions going. How many people was it?"

Nancy told her, and as she did so, she felt relieved — concentrating on the dispatcher's questions was so much easier than thinking about the blood and the pain.

"Just one that I'm aware of," she said.

"Did you see him?"

"Yes."

"Was he white? Black? Hispanic?"

"He was white. White with a black hat."

"How old?"

"I don't know."

The dispatcher couldn't make out Nancy's next set of answers. She sounded fainter now. Groaning for help. Moaning in pain. Fighting for her life, but growing weaker with each passing breath.

"Lord," she said once again. "I've been shot!"

"I know, ma'am. I can't imagine how bad it hurts. I just want you to stay on the phone."

The dispatcher glanced at the clock: Less than ninety seconds had passed since the call had come in. But help was still three or four minutes away from the house on Blue-bonnet Way.

At the two-minute mark, the dispatcher asked Nancy her name for the first time.

At the two-fifteen mark, she asked Nancy where she'd been shot.

At the three-minute mark, the dispatcher told Nancy that the police would be pulling up any minute.

Four minutes total had passed without the sound of sirens speeding toward Nancy, who was still moaning and praying to Jesus.

"If it's taking your energy to talk, you don't worry about it, okay?" the dispatcher told her. "I'm just going to sit here and make sure that they get to you."

"Please don't leave me; please don't go."

"Oh, yes, ma'am. I'm going to stay on the phone with you until they get there."

Of course the dispatcher would stay on the phone. If there was one thing the dispatcher had learned during her career with emergency services, it was that no one ever wanted to die alone — and from the sound of Nancy's breathing, the dispatcher was afraid that Nancy wouldn't be able to hold on much longer.

Finally, at the five-minute mark, help arrived.

"It's the police!"

"Yes, ma'am," the dispatcher said, and then she heard other voices, and Nancy's voice, saying, "Help me, help me," over and over again.

To Nancy, the dispatcher's voice seemed like the voice of an angel — an angel the Lord had sent to see her through.

She was still alive, still conscious, still on her feet. She even opened the front door for the two police officers and leaned against the doorjamb, looking like she'd stepped out of some horror movie as they sprinted up her driveway. But as the police officers ran up to Nancy, they saw something strange: The woman was smiling.

Looking at them, she saw two more angels. She'd been so scared — by the man, by the sight of her own, bloodied face in the mirror. She'd been praying so hard. All of her life, she had had so much faith. And now the Lord was rewarding her faith with a miracle. Nancy would live through this ordeal; she just knew it.

The sight of her standing there, bloodied, barely breathing, calling for help, praying to Jesus, and *smiling* — that was a sight neither of the officers would ever forget.

CHAPTER 28

Frank

Frank was still at the craps table when his
iPhone rang.

His daughter Ashley was on the line. Her
voice sounded strange.

"Dad," she said. "Mom's been shot."

Just like that. Matter-of-factly.

As if she'd been reporting the weather.

"What? Ashley, what are you *talking*
about?"

Suzanne looked up at Frank, startled. He
shushed her. On the phone, he heard Ashley's voice crack.

"Daddy, they shot her in the *head!*"

"Oh God," Frank said.

After all this time, Billie Earl Johnson had
finally come through.

"Ashley, what are you saying? Where's
Mommy now?"

"The police called my cell phone. I don't
know why they didn't call you. But, Daddy,

they *shot* her in the *head*!"

"What's her condition?"

Frank felt stupid saying the words: What's her *condition? It's shot in the head.* As they said in those lawyer shows Nancy would stay up late to watch: "Asked and answered." So Frank was surprised, even shocked, to hear what Ashley had to say next: "She's alive, Dad. The police say that she was conscious and on her feet when the ambulance arrived."

All of a sudden, Frank felt his world shift on its axis.

Alive!

Frank didn't know what to make of it. Billie Earl had told him that this plan was foolproof. But what were the odds that a woman who had been shot in the head would survive? It was something no one could have predicted.

There was a chance that Nancy would die in the night, before he could even get back to Texas. But Frank had to brace himself for worse scenarios.

If Nancy died, there'd be nothing to tie him to the shooting. That had been the whole point of hiring Billie Earl Johnson. But if Nancy lived, and identified the shooter, there was no telling where the police investigation might lead.

And even if that investigation went no-where, Nancy would still be there. One shooting could have been considered a one-off. A case of mistaken identity. Or a bur-glary gone wrong. But there was no way that Billie Earl, or anyone else, would ever get away with another attempt on Nancy's life.

Poison would have been the way to go. A car accident. A trip and a fall, maybe off the side of a mountain while hiking on some remote and romantic getaway.

Frank didn't know if he could have gone through with something like that. He didn't think he'd have been capable of hurting Nancy with his own hands. But anything — *anything* — would have been better than this.

Now he would still have to deal with Su-zanne in California. With her tears, and the fact that whatever happened, it looked like he couldn't be with her full-time for a while now.

And back home, he'd have to deal with Nancy. He'd have to look her in the eyes and lie, once again, about how much he loved her. About how sorry he was. But all he was really sorry about, at the moment, was that Billie Earl had screwed up so roy-ally.

Frank had never been as sorry about anything in his whole life.

CHAPTER 29

Nancy

While Frank was thinking about looking Nancy in the eyes and lying, Nancy was lying in the ICU at Parkland Memorial Hospital in Dallas.

She didn't even *have* eyes anymore. What Nancy had now was one eye and a gaping wound where the other one had been. She had shunts, bandages, tubes, and wires running every which way down her body.

But she was alive. She had to thank God for that. And her kids were there, in the next room, talking to a doctor who'd put a few scans of Nancy's brain up on the light board.

The bullet had entered just above Nancy's left eye, the doctor was saying. But instead of traveling straight through to her brain, it had taken a detour and traveled down her sinus cavity and throat before lodging in her right lung.

The lung had collapsed. The bullet was still there and would remain there for the foreseeable future. She'd be on a ventilator for a couple days, at least. Nancy's left eye was gone. Her throat was torn. She had extensive nerve damage.

That was the bad news. The good news was there was every indication that Nancy would live.

There was no brain damage — none at all.

Somebody had certainly been watching out for her. That was all Nancy needed to know at the moment — that, and the fact that she was *alive*. But other thoughts kept crowding her imagination. Time and again, she replayed her encounter with the man in the black baseball hat. Had she angered the man by handing him the takeout bag instead of her purse? Had she somehow brought the disaster upon herself?

Or was it something more than a disaster? Could the shooting have been a test, which Nancy's faith had allowed her to pass? Nancy didn't know why she'd been shot. But that didn't mean the shooting was senseless. Yes, it was a mystery. And Nancy knew mysteries could be full of meaning.

The Lord had spared her, and that was a miracle. After all, it had been His voice that had pulled her through. But what had He spared her *for*? That was the real mystery that Nancy would have to solve for herself. If she was going to walk away from this shooting, what was the lesson she would take with her?

Nancy wished that she could talk to Frank about it. Her husband, who had grown up in the church and had a gift for divining the good Lord's intentions.

Nancy's kids had assured her that Frank was on his way.

The last thing she thought before drifting off into a very deep sleep was "Florida's not so far away. He'll be on the first flight. We'll get through this together — just like we're meant to."

CHAPTER 30

Frank and Nancy

On Frank's first visit to the hospital, Nancy had a tube down her throat. But Frank stayed for a long time, holding her hand, comforting his children.

"Your mother's alive," he told the children. "Nothing else matters. Her shattered face can be reconstructed. Her body will heal."

The words felt surreal as he said them. The sound of his own voice was like something straight out of a dream. But what else could Frank have said? Ever since his affair — ever since he had started embezzling from his boss, Richard Raley — he'd been afraid of getting tangled up in his own lies. That's what had driven him toward Billie Earl Johnson. But Billie had failed, and the fear that Frank felt now cut more deeply. The more he talked, the more overwhelmed he became. It was as if he'd been swept overboard in some storm, and it was all he could do to tread water — keep his head above the surface until help arrived.

What help would look like, Frank didn't know. All he could do was keep lying for now.

"I'll stay right here by your mother's side," Frank said. "There's nowhere else I'd want to be."

For the next twenty minutes, Frank did his best to convey the notion that nothing could tear him and Nancy apart. That nothing ever had, or would. He'd gone home earlier that day, fetched his things, had all that he needed right there at the hospital. Now he would sleep in the armchair right at Nancy's feet, holding her hand for however long it took until the doctors told him they were out of the woods.

But just outside of Nancy's room, on his way to the bathroom, Frank found himself face-to-face with a Carrollton police officer. Startled, he couldn't help but take a step back. The police officer looked startled too. The Howards were friends of his, fellow parishioners at First Baptist Church.

How could this have happened to them?

Frank didn't know. *Couldn't* know. But, of course, he understood that the officer *did* have to ask him some questions. Nancy had finally fallen back asleep again, and if there was anything at all the officer thought Frank could help with, well then, he would bend over backward to help.

"Basic questions," the officer explained. "Anything you might have seen or heard around the neighborhood. Suspicious characters. That sort of thing."

"There's nothing," Frank said. "Nothing I can think of that would have led to this."

"Any break-ins that you're aware of?"

"There *was* that break-in over on Fairfield Drive, by the Parkway. But you know about that. And I don't know what that would have to do with Nancy. You're saying that none of the neighbors heard or saw anything at all?"

"It was raining pretty hard, Frank. Everyone was inside. Maybe someone will come forward. But at the moment it doesn't look like much more than an aggravated assault."

"Aggravated assault?" Frank asked, arching his eyebrows. Trying his best to look puzzled, he hoped the officer hadn't noticed his lips curl up into a smile. Anything that pointed the police away from him was a good thing, Frank reasoned.

"A botched robbery attempt or something of that nature. Maybe she came home and startled a burglar."

"Jesus. You saw what they did to her?"

"I wasn't there on the scene, Frank. But I want you to know that we're going to catch whoever did this. Now, I'm sorry to have to ask, but is there anything you can think of that Nancy herself could have done . . ."

"You know how Nancy is. She's so kindhearted, who knows who she might have answered the door for."

Frank's friend, the officer, nodded thoughtfully. Then, almost as an afterthought, and just for procedure's sake, he asked one last question:

"You weren't home when Nancy was shot?"

Frank shook his head: no.

"Okay, then. So, where were you?"

Frank hesitated. He'd told Nancy that he'd been in Florida. But lying to his wife was one thing. Lying to the police, in the wake of a shooting, could turn into something much worse. Weighing the word for a moment, he finally said, "California."

"Okay, Frank. That's fine. Of course, we'll have to interview you in a more formal setting, down at the station."

"Of course," Frank said. "Of course."

CHAPTER 31

Detective Wall

Down at the station, Detective Michael Wall led Frank Howard down a long hallway, toward an interrogation room.

Getting Frank down to the station had been little more than a formality. The fact that he was the victim's husband made him an automatic suspect. But the police knew Frank had been in Tahoe on the night of the shooting. And back in Carrollton, where the Howards had lived for years and years, everyone knew Frank to be an upstanding, churchgoing family man.

The most that the detective hoped for now was that Frank would be able to fill in some background, remember a detail or two that would generate some sort of lead.

"Can you update me on your wife's condition?" the detective asked. "Tell me what the doctors said?"

"Yes," Frank said. "Actually it sounds very

bad when you say it: 'Somebody was shot in the head.' But actually, it's very, very good."

Nancy's injuries could have been so much worse, Frank told the detective.

"There's no brain damage. None of that. She'll lose her eye, but from there it will be cosmetic stuff."

"Is there anything you know of — did she have problems with anybody?"

"No, no," Frank insisted. "Absolutely not. But Nancy can be real giving and . . . and real open. She'll open our door to a stranger, invite him inside. Pick a hitchhiker up and go out of her way to drop him at his location. A month ago, someone came to our door. They just needed money to get a hotel room 'cause their car had broken down —"

"They came to your house?"

"To the house, yeah. They came to the front door. And Nancy told them — she's got a good heart — she said that she'd help them *find* a hotel room."

"You think she might have opened the door for someone on the night of the shooting?"

"I don't know," Frank said. "I wish to God that I did know."

"And our understanding is you were not

there on the night of the shooting."

"No, sir, I was not. I travel a lot for work. I did text with Nancy and emailed with her that day. I know that she had a ladies' lunch at our church."

"You texted with her right before the shooting?"

"Yes, sir. That's my understanding."

"And just to confirm that, would you mind if we ran an analysis on your cell phone?"

"Not at all. And if there's anything else I can do . . . if it gets to the point where I can offer a reward, anything at all, I'll be happy to do it."

Frank looked down at his hands. He didn't want to seem overeager. But this seemed just short of the line, and he was relieved when he looked back up and saw the detective smiling at him.

"Thank you," Detective Wall said as he took Frank's iPhone and placed it in a yellow envelope. "If it gets to the point where we've exhausted our leads, that's another step we could take. Obviously, money can prompt people to give information."

"Yes, sir," Frank said.

"In my experience," Wall added as he shook Frank's hand, "money makes people do all sorts of things."

CHAPTER 32

Frank and Nancy

Nancy had been unconscious for two days in a row, but her doctors had assured Frank that she was not in a coma. Her body needed all the strength it could get to recuperate. It knew that it had to sleep. *Nancy* might not have known it, but she was fighting hard — and she was going to make it through to the other side. In a few days, they hoped, she could even go home.

What could Frank do but sigh and sit in Nancy's hospital room, watching the ventilator move up and down, up and down? When the kids arrived that day, they formed a prayer circle around their mother. "Heavenly Father," they said, and just then they saw Nancy's right eye — her remaining eye — twitch under its eyelid.

The very next day she was fully awake.

Then, with the breathing tube out, she was talking. But as soon as the kids left the room, Frank told her that he had a few things of his own to say.

The past twenty-four hours had been grueling for him. It wasn't just the long hours he'd spent at the hospital. It was that Michael Wall and the Carrollton police had found something he had not expected them to find on his cell phone.

They'd found out about Suzanne and the affair Frank had been having.

He'd been so careful up to that point. He'd used disposable phones for every conversation he'd had with Billie Earl and with Billie's associates. And it wasn't like he'd put Suzanne's *name* in his iPhone. All this while her contact info had read "S. Tahoe Cell."

"South Tahoe," if anyone had thought to ask.

But Frank had not expected anyone to ask.

Certainly not the police.

What Frank *had* expected was that the police would make sure he'd texted and emailed with Nancy, like they said they would. That they'd see he hadn't been anywhere *near* Carrollton on the night that Nancy had been shot.

In other words, he'd taken the cops at their word.

But as far as Frank was concerned, the

cops had not been honest with him. Detective Wall had checked the rest of his phone logs as well. He'd checked the rest of Frank's texts, including his texts with Suzanne.

He'd seen cell phone pictures of Frank and Suzanne together — on vacation, at football games.

Detective Wall had even put in a call to the FBI, which gave him Suzanne's full name, age, and occupation.

Then Wall had called *Suzanne* — actually *called* her. And while Suzanne had confirmed that Frank had been with her in Tahoe on the night that Nancy had been shot, it was not quite the alibi Frank would have wished for.

What Frank had told the police was that he'd been in California on business. Now Detective Wall had caught him in a lie. Not a lie that linked him, in any way, with Billie Earl Johnson or Nancy's shooting. But a lie he couldn't counter, given the information the police had gotten ahold of.

The only thing Frank could do now was stay as far as he could ahead of that lie.

And that meant he *had* to tell Nancy about his affair.

CHAPTER 33

Nancy

For the second time in a week, Nancy was in shock.

She stared at Frank in disbelief as he wept and begged for her forgiveness and swore — *swore* — that it was nothing he ever wanted to happen and nothing that would ever happen again.

Didn't this man understand what she'd been through? Didn't he understand how cruel he'd been — and how cruel it was to tell her *now,* when she was helpless and bandaged and looking like three hundred miles of bad road? She almost *died.* And now Nancy felt like Frank was trying to kill her. He might as well be trying to choke her. That's how hard it was for Nancy to breathe as she listened to Frank talk and talk.

First, he talked about how weak he'd been. How lost he's felt ever since the children left home.

Then he talked about Suzanne and how she meant nothing to him. She'd pursued him, Frank told Nancy. And it'd been so long since he'd been pursued by a woman.

Frank had been flattered by it, nothing more. He's vain, as well as weak. Girls and greed had always been his weaknesses. He was a sinner; he knew it. But what he needed for Nancy to know was that it'd all been just a fling.

It wasn't that other woman he loved. It was her flattery.

Seeing Nancy like this was what's shown him the need to come clean about the affair, Frank told her. It'd made him realize how much he treasured her.

Only now did he understand the true value of the twenty-eight years they'd spent together.

In sickness and health, he said. Isn't that what it's really about?

Hitting his stride now, Frank began to cry. He needed Nancy to believe him now. He needed for her to need him. Because if she needed him, she'd never suspect that he was behind her shooting.

And so, Frank told Nancy that he knew how much time it would take to fix this. He knew Nancy might never forgive him. All he could do was ask her now — now that he's being *completely* honest — could she try? He'd come back to her, decided that he'd never want to just throw their marriage away. Maybe Nancy could find it in her heart to do the same thing?

But Nancy was crying as well. Crying out of pity for Frank and how foolish he'd been. Crying for having finally learned the reason for all the distance she'd felt in her marriage — for the way Frank had taken to acting around her.

Crying because she was wondering, even now, if she had done something to push Frank away. Crying because now that she *knew,* she was wondering if there was a way through the ordeal.

And so, as she cried, Nancy's disbelief began to turn into acceptance — something like acceptance, at least. Something that she'd have to live with and pray on.

She never had had it in her to hate.

Even now, with Frank having done this terrible thing, she had to admit that she loved him. She couldn't imagine what she'd do without him. And it didn't cross Nancy's mind for one second — would not cross her mind for one million years — that Frank had it in him, for years now, to do something far more terrible.

■ ■ ■ ■

PART SIX:
ONE WEEK AFTER
THE SHOOTING

■ ■ ■ ■

CHAPTER 34

Frank

The week that had passed since the shooting was just the time it'd taken for Frank's life to change drastically.

Nancy was home for good now, though there were still several doctor's visits a week, and Frank had been playing the role of the dutiful nursemaid — changing her bandages, helping her in and out of the bath. In the downtime, he cooked for Nancy, fetched snacks and drinks. Most of the time, she seemed very grateful. And when the pain became too much for Nancy to bear, she still didn't *take it out* on Frank — not really. Even though she still cried over the shooting and, even more often, over Frank's affair, she seemed to have forgiven him. She said as much the first time she came home from the hospital: "If the good Lord had it in his heart to forgive," she told him, "I have to find it in mine."

But the more forgiving Nancy was, the more resentful of her Frank seemed to become. It wasn't that he felt guilty, exactly. It was that she was a walking, talking reminder of the trouble Frank had gotten himself into.

It'd been a week, too, since Frank had seen Suzanne — a week full of furtive phone calls, which he'd had to sneak out of the house for. A week's worth of guilt trips and accusations from a mistress he'd started to tire of, but couldn't let go of, in part because he was afraid of the questions she'd ask.

Frank had done nothing to tip Suzanne off about his plans to do away with Nancy — in that regard, he'd been so very careful. Suzanne would never suspect him of planning an actual *murder.* But together, Frank and Suzanne had spent more money than any small-town accountant like Frank could have earned. Suzanne had never asked Frank about it directly. Then again, she'd gotten used to the very comfortable lifestyle that Frank had provided her. If he were to cut her off, there's no telling what questions she'd ask.

Suzanne wasn't stupid. And, Frank knows, she wasn't above making threats.

"Honey," he said when Suzanne called for

the sixth time that week and asked why he was there in Texas and not with her. "Where else could I be? Nancy's been *shot.* We're lucky she's alive!"

"Oh, Frank," said Suzanne. "How am I supposed to compete with *that*?"

If there's any good news, it's that it'd been a few days since Frank had heard from Michael Wall, the detective who's handing the investigation. The last time they spoke, Wall assured him that Carrollton PD would track down Nancy's assailant. But Wall didn't seem to have any actual *leads* — and that's fine as far as Frank was concerned. There were no witnesses to Nancy's crime. Nancy's own description of the assailant was vague: a white man in his twenties. Strong jaw. Facial hair. That's pretty much half the population of the Dallas metropolitan area. And, Frank knew, that wasn't even where the assailant was from.

But if Frank was at peace with the investigation, he couldn't find peace within himself. Sometimes, Frank couldn't help but snap at Nancy. And even when he did manage to hold everything in, his wife told him that he seemed distracted.

What could Frank say to that? He *was* distracted. While Nancy had been watching her shows, Frank had been bent over his laptop, glued to the spreadsheets he'd been fiddling with for months. His old book-keeper — the one who had the nerve to ask about certain *discrepancies* in his books — was long gone. Frank let her go, he told Nancy. Ever since he told his boss, Richard Raley, that he'd have to cut back on his travel, there'd been a lot less work coming in. But what that meant now was that Frank had to do the books himself. And no matter how hard he tried to finagle the numbers, he'd siphoned too much money out of Raley's accounts to make it all square in the spreadsheets.

Night after night, he stayed up in his home office, his face lit by the dim glow of the laptop. Night after night, the numbers didn't square. And then, one night, he logged on and found that he'd been locked out of one of his accounts. He tried one password, and then another. Then he tried another account.

He *needed* those accounts. There were still millions of dollars to account for, to hide. He typed in more passwords — every one he could remember.

Still no go. Frank's chest tightened a bit. His throat went dry. But there wasn't much more he could do in the moment. Nancy's calling for him again, asking for a refill on her sweet tea.

CHAPTER 35

Detective Wall

Michael Wall stirred his third cup of coffee as he looked at a sketch of the criminal he was supposed to be catching.

Nancy Howard's instructions to the forensic artist had been white male, square jaw, facial hair, dark baseball cap.

It could have been anyone's face. But it was better than nothing.

Next, Wall took out the folder of photographs taken at the scene of the shooting. The garage door's still open. In front of Nancy's parked car — a blue, late-model Buick — there's an overturned black plastic bin that is covered in Nancy's blood.

Inside the house, there's more blood, on the walls, on the floor. It looks like the aftermath of a massacre.

There are photographs, too, of a nearby Dumpster — one that Carrollton PD had discovered after running a trace on Nancy's cell phone. The shooter had dumped Nancy's purse there, without taking her wallet, her cell phone, or keys. But, Detective Wall noted, the purse *had* been rifled through. Nancy's driver's license had been removed and discarded separately from the rest of her wallet's contents.

The detective set a photograph of the license aside, opened his case notes, and underlined a few things that he had learned: "Shooter *did not* know Nancy Howard personally. Did not take car keys, wallet, or money. But *checked against license* to make sure of her identity and did this *after* the shooting."

Michael Wall had known for a week now that Frank Howard had lied to Nancy about his whereabouts on the night of the shooting. Nancy had thought that Frank had been in Tampa. But then, *of course* Howard lied. He was having an affair. Like all cheating husbands, he'd have lied to anyone — said anything — to cover his tracks. The fact of that lie was less conclusive than the fact that Frank's mistress, Suzanne Leontieff, confirmed Frank's alibi, placing him in Tahoe on the night of the shooting.

Still, it didn't add up. A cheating husband. A shooter who had to confirm he'd shot the right woman based on her license photo. A professional hit, in that the would-be killer had acted in cold blood, shooting Nancy Howard in the forehead while looking straight into her eyes. But a hit that had been botched, as only an amateur could have botched it?

If not for the surveillance tapes from First Baptist Church, Detective Wall would have been nowhere. But what those tapes had revealed was that a silver car had followed Nancy Howard's Buick into the church parking lot.

When Nancy had parked, the silver car had parked, too, just a few spots away. When Nancy entered the church, the silver car drove away — only to return one hour later. Then a man had stepped out and walked into the church, where another surveillance camera captured him on his way into and out of a restroom.

None of the surveillance footage was anywhere near the quality Wall would have wished it to be. The detective had scanned it again and again and still couldn't make out the silver car's plates. But grainy as the footage was, it *did* show the man's hooded sweatshirt, his blue jeans and black sneakers. It showed a *dark baseball cap* that all but covered his face. And it showed the thing that had cemented Detective Wall's belief that Nancy Howard had been targeted — singled out — for extermination.

A few minutes after the man in the baseball cap had exited the men's room, Nancy had exited the church. Outside, she'd walked through the rain back to her car. And when Nancy had pulled her car out of the church parking lot, the silver car had pulled out behind her and followed her into the street.

In the police department's kitchen, where Wall had gone for his fourth cup of coffee, the other cops were incredulous.

"A hit man, Detective?"

"That's what it looks like to me. I don't have a confirmed suspect, or motive. I don't have concrete evidence that would tie the victim's husband in with the case. What I *do* have is footage that tells me the victim was tailed. I have her driver's license — a license that the shooter checked and discarded, *after performing the hit.* I have a screenshot of a man who basically matches the victim's description, right in the church that he followed her from."

"Good enough to run through the database?"

"No, not nearly. But with one more lead, we could crack this case open."

By the time Michael Wall had had his fifth and final cup of coffee for the day, the news had spread through the station: A shooter — a *hit man* — working right under their noses in Carrollton. The cops could hardly believe it. Nothing like this had ever happened in Carrollton before. But Wall had a good reputation. He was thorough and levelheaded. And on his way out of the office that evening, he finally caught a break.

"Detective?"

Wall turned around and saw Bethany Wright, a Carrollton PD officer who worked night patrol and raised two teenage boys by herself during the day.

"Officer, what can I do for you?"

"Detective, I heard about your break in the Howard case. It was a targeted hit?"

"That's what it looks like, Bethany. They tossed the victim's purse but took the driver's license out of it first."

"Checking to make sure they'd shot the right woman?"

"Can't see another reason for someone to do that," the detective says.

"Maybe I should have mentioned this sooner," says the officer. "But a few weeks, maybe a few months ago, I booked a kid from East Texas. A meth head. I'll go find the paperwork for you. But what I remember about him is this: He wouldn't stop talking. And I'll check my notes, but the thing that stuck in my mind was he told me he'd come to town to kill somebody."

"You don't say," says the detective. "Well, you've got my full attention."

"Now, most of what he said made no sense *at all.* He was just rambling and rambling. His brains were fried. A meth head, like I said. But he was just a kid, not much older than my own sons. I didn't make much of it at the time."

"And you checked this kid's record?"

"I did. It was clean. So I let him sleep it off in the cell and we let him go the next morning. But, Detective, there's one more thing I remember."

"I'm listening, Bethany."

"He actually used the word 'hit man.' "

"Okay. We will certainly be looking into that. And, Bethany?"

"Yes, sir?"

"In the future, please feel free to come to me with anything like this. Anything at all."

"Of course, sir. I'm sorry I didn't bring it up earlier."

"Well, you're probably right and it's probably nothing, so there's nothing for you to feel sorry about. But in the meantime, why don't you go and get all your paperwork on the kid. I'll stick around and we'll look over that report together."

CHAPTER 36

Billie

Bethany Wright's memories of the methed-out kid matched up neatly with what she wrote down on the night of Dustin's arrest. It was right there, in the report: "I came to Carrollton to do a hit," Dustin had told the officer. "That's what I do. I'm a hit man."

But Dustin's record, up to that night, had been clean. If he *was* a hit man, he must have been the most careful hit man in Texas. And nothing else in the report indicated that Dustin was in the least bit careful. Detective Wall told the officer he would have done the same thing: arrested the kid, hoped that it put the fear of God into him, and let him go.

All the same, it was quite the coincidence. The detective still thought it was certainly worth looking into.

But the next day, when he followed up with Nancy Howard, Detective Wall hit a snag. Holding Dustin's mug shot up to the light in her kitchen, the detective couldn't help but notice that Nancy trembled slightly as she said she didn't recognize him as the shooter.

"That's too bad," the detective told her. "We could have cracked this case right on the spot."

"I'm sorry," Nancy said, and for the second time in as many days, Detective Wall said, "Nothing to be sorry about."

He meant it too. For the detective, Nancy's inability to ID the suspect wasn't entirely conclusive. After all, the surveillance tape from First Baptist showed *two* men in the silver car that followed Nancy in and out of the church parking lot. Detective Wall made a few marks in his notepad. Back at the station, he put a call in to the police department in Dustin's town, a hundred miles away from Carrollton.

But before the cops there could get back to him, Wall got an intriguing phone call.

An investigator in Denton, Texas, called to say that an inmate at the Denton jail claimed to have information about Nancy Howard's shooting.

The inmate turned out to be Billie Earl Johnson — a petty criminal who was very familiar with the inner workings of Texas's criminal justice system.

"I'll level with you," Johnson said when Detective Wall drove up to Denton to meet him. "I've got a reputation of being a bad-ass. I mean, everybody's claiming me to be tough and bad. I ain't claiming to be tough and bad. I'm mean. I'm *mean*. What that means is, if you jump on me, I'm going to hurt you."

Sitting there in his prison jumpsuit, covered in tattoos, Billie looked every bit like the hard case he'd become.

"I'm forty-nine years old," he said. "I done been in the pen a total of fifteen years. I got grandkids that I want to spend the rest of my life with. I want to be free. And I want out this weekend."

In exchange for his freedom, he said, Billie was ready to give up the hit team. The ball's in Wall's court, Billie told the detective. And the detective had to admit, Billie knew things about the shooting that only someone with some sort of involvement would know: the make and model of Nancy's Buick. Her address and the basic layout of her house in Carrollton.

"If y'all want this murder solved," Billie said, "y'all need to work with me. 'Cause I ain't playing."

Detective Wall knew that Billie could not

have been the shooter. The timeline put him in jail on the night of the attack on Nancy Howard. So whatever it was that Billie had to share had better be good.

"You've got to give me some more," Wall told him. "What I need to know from you now is not just the *who* and the *how* but the *why*. Why would someone want to shoot this woman, Nancy Howard?"

Billie leaned back in the interrogation room's office chair. He's got his arms splayed out, arrogantly, across the armrests. With his reading glasses pushed up high on his forehead, he looks a bit like a college professor who's gone to seed. And he's still acting as if he's holding the high card — the ace in the hole.

"I'll level with you, Billie," the detective said. "I don't think this woman deserves what happened —"

"No, she sure didn't —" Billie interrupted.

"— and she deserves a little bit of justice."

"Yep, and she'll get it. But I want my back scratched too."

"Then tell us *why* this thing happened."

"I was laying on the couch and the phone rang," Billie began. At first, it sounded like a tangent — a story about a man named John who first contacted Billie around 2009.

But before long, the story started to come into focus.

"How he got my information, I don't know," Billie said. "He said, 'You don't know me.' Told me his name was John. Said, 'I don't know you, but I caught word that you might be the one to do a job for me.' He wanted it done as an accident so it wouldn't come on him. Like a carjacking, purse-snatching accident. Now, I'm not gonna go kill nobody. But if this man John wants to throw his money away, you're damn sure I'm going to take it."

"What does that mean, Billie?"

"I strung him along and strung him along. For years. This man John drove a Lexus. He carried tens of thousands of dollars in cash. He had money to burn."

"How many conversations did you have with this John regarding this getting done?"

"Numerous."

"More than ten?"

"Yeah."

"More than twenty?"

"Fifty. Sixty."

Detective Wall wrote it all down in his notebook. Then, flipping back a few pages, he looked over the notes that he'd made after reading Dustin's arrest report, back at the station.

"Mr. John," Dustin had told Officer Bethany Wright. She'd written it down in the arrest report that she'd shown the detective.

"Mr. John" was the name of the man Dustin claimed to have come to Carrollton to meet.

"Billie," said the detective. "I want to ask you about Dustin —"

"Shit," Billie interrupted him. "That's my son-in-law," he said, confusing the word for "stepson."

"You're married, Billie?"

"No, but his mother and I are together."

"And do you think Dustin might have had something to do with this shooting?"

"Dustin? He's so stupid he don't know how to put antifreeze in a truck. He don't know nothin' about nothin'."

Billie knew he was skirting the edge: He'd told the cops he knew who the shooter was. And he knew that Dustin was there that night. Still he thought he could walk the fine line, give the cops just enough information without implicating his girlfriend's son.

"And if we were to have a few words with him?" asked the detective.

"Be my guest," said Billie. Then his face hardened. "But you'll be barking up the wrong tree. Y'all want it, I'm the one who's got it. I'll give it to you in a golden basket.

164

But I'm not giving up nothing until I've got something solid on my end. I'll *die* with it."

Sitting there, grinning his arrogant grin, Billie did not understand that he'd given the police so much already: that by admitting he knew who the shooter was he'd all but implicated himself in the shooting.

For the moment, Detective Wall was not about to let on.

CHAPTER 37

Dustin

Down at the Smith County Sherriff's Office, two hours outside of Carrollton, Dustin did very little to dispel Billie Johnson's sorry description of him.

He really did seem too dumb to change the antifreeze in a truck.

There's still a part of Michael Wall that can't believe Frank would hire someone so stupid to do Nancy in. But, in the course of the week, a few things had come into focus for the detective: Billie's description of "Mr. John" matched Frank Howard perfectly. Then there's Frank's full name, which turned out to be *John Franklin Howard.* And now there's Dustin.

Wall had spent a full day talking to Dustin, waiting for him to calm down, winning his trust, and waiting for the right moment to show him a photograph of Frank Howard.

When that moment came, Dustin bolted out of his chair.

"Yeah!" he said. "That's Mr. John!"

"You're a good kid," the detective told Dustin. "You've got yourself messed up in a little thing, but you're a good kid."

But when Dustin looked back up at Wall, his eyes were wild. It'd been a week since the shooting, and several days now since he'd had any real sleep. First, there'd been the mountain of meth that he'd done. Then the meth had run out — which had been even worse. He'd gotten nauseous and sweaty, dry-mouthed, paranoid. And that was before he'd opened his door to the Carrollton detective waiting outside.

Now, at the station, Dustin couldn't stop shaking. He'd been talking to the cops for hours now. Talking in circles and crying, lost in his own lies. All week, he'd been afraid that his mom's boyfriend, Billie, would find out that he and Michael had failed at the job — find out that, although she'd been shot in the head, Nancy Howard was alive and out of the hospital. If Billie found out, there'd be hell to pay. And no matter how much meth he smoked, Dustin knew that it was a matter of *when* and not if.

He'd been so scared, he hadn't even

thought of the cops. But Detective Wall was even-tempered, encouraging. Dealing with him, in the moment, had to have been better than dealing with Billie Earl Johnson down the line.

Even if it wasn't, Dustin did not see that he had any choice. And so he talked, and talked, and kept on talking. He talked about all the money that he, and Billie, and other folks in Ben Wheeler had burned through — astronomical sums — but when the detective pressed him, Dustin said, no, it's all true. Tens of thousands. Hundreds of thousands, all the way into the millions.

"One time, it must have been eight thousand dollars blew off the hood of my car," Dustin said.

"Did you go back to get it?"

"Nah. We all knew there was more where it came from."

Dustin talked about how stupid they all thought Mr. John was to keep paying and about how sorry he felt now for Nancy Howard.

"She didn't do nothing wrong," Dustin told the detective. "She's a Christian woman, dude."

"Who shared with you that she's a Christian woman?"

"John did."

Then Dustin started talking about all of John's plans to murder the woman: in her hotel room, during some convention. In a restaurant parking lot. At home, while scrapbooking with her friends. It would be all right to kill her friends, John had told him, as long as he got Nancy for sure. It would be all right to burn the house down, too, as long as Nancy was inside it.

"Sometimes he'd say 'use a baseball bat.' Sometimes he'd say 'use a gun.' The time he told me to 'just burn her house down,' Mr. John laughed."

There's a part of the detective that didn't *want* to believe it. He didn't want to believe that a man like Frank Howard could *be* Mr. John. That a man — a *preacher's kid,* for God's sake — could do such evil, and do it to those he was closest to. He did not want to believe that such a man could have lived, worked, and worshipped right there in Carrollton, a town full of god-fearing, law-abiding, decent, and kindhearted people.

But, with the facts right there in front of him, the detective *did* believe it. He knew that John Franklin Howard would rot in hell for what he did to his wife, Nancy. And before he did, the detective hoped he'd feel the full weight of the judicial system in Texas — feel it hard, and for a long time, like the wrath of the God that Frank Howard betrayed when he first put his mind to violating the commandments against murder and adultery.

CHAPTER 38

Nancy

The bandage over Nancy's left eye was smaller now. She was steadier on her feet, getting around the house and even out in the yard, where she sat in a wooden lawn chair, leafing through magazines while Frank was away at the office.

It had been a few days now since Frank had gone back to work full-time. Nancy was learning what it's like to be lonely again, except she was lonelier now for having had Frank at home since the shooting, taking care of her around the clock. He'd spoiled her, Nancy thought, with all of this care and attentiveness. Of course, some of it *had* to come down to the guilt he felt over falling for some other woman. But whoever that woman might be, it's Nancy that Frank had finally chosen. He'd assured her, many times over, swearing to God that he'd put an end to the affair.

Still, Nancy thought, if she could spend just five minutes inside of Frank's head. What had drawn her to him in the first place was how open he was. She used to read him like an open book — every hope and dream that he'd ever had was written right there on his face. And over the years, most of those hopes and those dreams had come true. But somewhere along the way, the book of Frank had snapped shut.

Nancy did not understand it at all.

Sighing, she got up from the lawn chair, shuffled back into the house, and lay down on the living room sofa. The garage and downstairs hallway smelled like fresh paint — it'd taken two coats to cover the bloodstains. Nancy was too attached to this house, where she raised her children, to ask Frank to move. But she didn't go downstairs anymore. Frank did their laundry now, dropped her off at the front door after outings before pulling into the garage. But attentive as he had been, Frank couldn't do everything. He was helpless in the kitchen, for instance. So tonight, on his way home, he'd stop by Cane Rosso, the brick-oven pizza place, to pick up some Bolognese and a couple of marinara pies. Ashley, their daughter, was coming to dinner, and pizza had always been her favorite food.

Smiling at the thought of it, Nancy drifted off.

When she woke up, Nancy didn't know what time it was. She didn't remember falling asleep on the sofa. She didn't remember her dreams. But it must have been evening because Frank was home, and Ashley too. Nancy heard their voices, coming from the kitchen, and smelled the good Italian food.

"Honey?" she calleds out.

No answer. She hears Frank's laugh, and Ashley's. They always did have their own, private language. So much has changed for them these past few weeks, Nancy thinks. But the most important things stayed the same.

"Honey?" she called again, louder this time.

"I'll be right there," Frank answered, but Nancy didn't hear him. Someone was knocking at their front door.

"Frank? *Frank?* I hear someone knocking."

"I'll get it," Frank hollered back.

Outside, Detective Michael Wall and two Carrollton police officers were waiting with an arrest warrant.

"Frank, what *is* this?"

Nancy was standing in the vestibule, looking into her husband's eyes as one of the officers put him in handcuffs.

"You have the right to remain silent," the other officer said.

"Honey," Frank said, "I'll just have to go down to the station. Answer some questions. I'll be back tonight."

"But, Frank, they've got you in handcuffs!"

"I know, hon," Frank said. But he was as white as a ghost, and when he said, "I'll sort this out," his voice broke.

Nancy looked over at Ashley, who was covering her mouth with her hand. Then she looked down at her own hands, which were trembling.

The shock of the shooting . . . the shock of finding out about Frank's affair . . . and now this? Feeling terribly weak, Nancy put a hand on the sofa to steady herself.

She didn't know how much more she could take.

"Officer?" she said, turning to the man who looked like the officer in charge. "This can't be happening. There must be some sort of mistake."

"Ma'am," the man said. "I'm sorry to have to do this in front of you and your daughter. But I'd advise you to call your lawyer. And I'd think about calling your minister too."

174

Nancy didn't know *what* to do. She looked at her daughter again and saw her crying.

"Come here, babe," Nancy said. But Ashley just stood there, shaking.

"We got through the past few weeks," Frank told his daughter. "The Howards can get through anything."

"Daddy?" she said.

The look he gave her broke Nancy's heart. But a moment later Frank was gone, the police were gone, and the house on Bluebonnet Way was quiet again.

■ ■ ■ ■

PART SEVEN:
AUGUST 2014

■ ■ ■ ■

CHAPTER 39

Frank

It had been nearly two years now that Frank had been out on bail.

"The wheels of justice grind slowly," the judge at the bond hearing had told him. "But, Mr. Howard, you'll find that once they get started, they grind very effectively."

Now that his murder trial was starting, Frank was afraid that he'd find out the hard way. But it wasn't as if the past two years had been some sort of picnic.

Days after his arrest for soliciting the murder of Nancy Howard, Frank was sued by his boss, Richard Raley. Frank's lawyer, Arch McColl, had called the charges "preposterous." But Frank had known better — and, in the end, a panel of arbitrators had ruled against him, in the amount of $8.5 million in actual and putative damages.

"Good luck getting that money," is what

Frank had thought at the time. "It's long gone."

He decided that he would file his own suit against Raley. And, of course, Frank had even bigger problems to solve.

First, he and Nancy had had to tell the children about his affair. There was no hiding it after the arrest, not once the news channels had gotten ahold of Detective Wall's warrant.

Then Frank had had to contend with Nancy.

At first, she didn't believe the charges. Nancy simply could not imagine a world in which Frank would *want* her dead, much less a world in which he would actually *act* on the notion. Lying in bed late at night, she'd look over at Frank and try to stop her thoughts from spinning. But once the thought had been planted, it grew and grew, until it had overwhelmed all the others: Could this whole business, insane as it sounded, be true? Once she had caught herself wondering, she couldn't stop. And once that happened, Nancy found herself in a dark place. A place where, for the first time, her faith in the Lord and her love for her husband seemed like they would fail her. Filing for divorce was the only thing that she *could* do, she'd said with tears in

180

her eyes. Try as she might, she couldn't see another solution.

It had split the family apart, and not just in the obvious ways. The more convinced Nancy became in regards to Frank's involvement in the shooting, the more convinced their daughters seemed to be in regards to Frank's innocence. Learning about their father's affair had been hard. But the leap from love affair to murder plot seemed, to them, absurd. Like Nancy, in those first few days after Frank's arrest, the kids couldn't imagine a world in which their father would do such a thing.

Unlike Nancy's, their faith seemed to be shatterproof.

It was the one true comfort Frank had had during those long months leading up to the trial. No matter what, his kids stood by him. And when the time came for Brianna to marry her fiancé, Nancy had written the court and asked that the conditions of Frank's bail be amended so that he could attend the ceremony and walk his daughter down the aisle.

Suzanne was gone, out of Frank's life for good. He hadn't seen her since she'd driven him to the airport on the night of Nancy's shooting. She hadn't called him — not even once — after reading about his arrest. Suzanne's daughters had not even known that Frank was married. Now they knew everything, including the fact that Frank had become the prime suspect in the attempted murder of his own wife.

Meanwhile, Billie Earl Johnson was sitting in jail, preparing to testify against Frank. In exchange, he'd gotten what seemed to him like a good deal from the government: A twenty-four-year sentence for drug trafficking, but no charges in relation to the plot to kill Nancy Howard. He'd have to give up some friends, for sure. But then Billie wondered — did he really have any friends?

Caged in his cell, Billie had had plenty of time to think. He thought about Stacey, and Dustin, her idiot son. He thought about Michael Lorence, the stranger Dustin had glared at, back in that biker bar in East Texas. At some point, Lorence had been a cell mate of Michael Speck's. A man close enough to trust, but far enough from Billie to keep suspicions at rest, in case he had been caught.

But Lorence had not been caught. And unlike Dustin, he'd actually had it in him to go through with the shooting. He had gone to Nancy Howard's house, along with Speck. And there, in the Howards' garage, he had pulled the trigger. The best part had

been, he and Speck had agreed to the shooting for a measly $5,000 a piece.

The worst part, of course, was that they
had failed to actually *kill* Nancy Howard.

As for Frank, he'd done all that he could to
win in the court of public opinion. He still
had friends in Carrollton. Men and women
who knew him from church, knew his
children, knew in their hearts that he'd
never be capable of such a crime. They
pinned the blame on burglars, vagrants,
spree killers — anything made more sense
than the idea that Frank had set out to kill
his own wife. Those friends had packed the
court at his bond hearing, ready to testify
about his good character. They were why he
was free now, Frank supposed. While out on
bond, he'd gone on the news shows, licked
his lips, and cried. His daughters had come
onto the programs, too, speaking in their
father's defense. Even Nancy, who'd finally
landed on the side of believing in Frank's
involvement, was careful not to come out
and say it on camera.

"I believe he had relationships with the
kind of people who would do something like
this," she'd say. "But I'm going to let the
jury make the decision on whether he called
the shot."

Now, with the trial set to begin, Frank's lawyers told him they were hopeful. He was an upstanding, churchgoing man. Most of the witnesses lined up against him were criminals, testifying in exchange for more lenient sentences during their own upcoming trials. You never knew, they told Frank. But his chances were solid.

Even at his most hopeful, Frank wasn't so sure.

CHAPTER 40

Frank

In court, Frank's lawyers argued that Frank himself had been the victim in a long series of terribly unfortunate events. Far from trying, and failing, to orchestrate his wife's murder, he'd found himself caught in a blackmailing scheme. Way back in 2009, they argued, Billie Earl Johnson had found out about Frank's affair with Suzanne Leontieff. Billie had tried to blackmail him over it. Heck, Billie *had* blackmailed Frank, to the tune of hundreds of thousands, even millions, of dollars. He'd bled Frank dry in exchange for his silence. Then, when Frank finally stopped paying, Billie had taken his revenge and hired an accomplice to shoot Nancy Howard.

It was a good story, Frank thought. Nancy herself was disgusted.

And then their children — Ashley, Jay, and Brianna — stood up to take their places in the witness stand.

Frank had his failings; it was true. All three of his children had learned that by now. Hearing about his affair had shocked, even shattered, them — if they hadn't known their own father, what *did* they know?

What could they be sure of?

The answer turned out to be simple: The children were sure of Frank's innocence — they *had* to be — because if Frank was guilty, their world no longer made sense. And so, one by one, they testified in his favor.

"My family foundation is built on God, faith, and grace," Jay said, turning all the way in the witness chair to face the jury. "Since Jesus has given me grace, I ask that you do the same for my father."

Brianna called him a "great man," spoke about how much she loved him and how he'd been there for her for all twenty-three years of her life.

Ashley took a more pragmatic approach. Frank had always been there for the family, she said, even during these last two years since his arrest. His alimony checks for Nancy never came late. In fact, he was still Nancy's main source of income. "What benefit is there to putting him away?" she asked.

■ ■ ■ ■

Suzanne Leontieff took the stand, too, during the first week of the trial. It was the first time that Frank had seen her in almost two years. She told the jury she really had loved Frank, and really had expected him to leave Nancy for her. She'd planned out their whole life together — although, Suzanne had to admit, she'd gotten fed up toward the end with Frank's endless excuses. But she also knew in her heart that Frank was a good husband. She described the way he'd collapsed, sobbing, after learning that Nancy had been shot.

There was no way Suzanne could have imagined that Frank was involved in the attempted murder.

Frank had mixed feelings about Suzanne's testimony. It did nothing to cement the idea that he was a committed family man. He wished the woman wouldn't giggle so much. It was unseemly, given the circumstances. But Frank wasn't on trial for the affair — a fact that his lawyers had stressed repeatedly in their opening address to the jury — and, overall, he guessed that Suzanne had done more to help than to harm him.

That was something he could not have

said about other witnesses called by the prosecution.

Sober now, after a long stint in prison, Billie Earl Johnson was more coherent than Frank had ever seen him be out in the world. Up on the witness stand, he put on a real performance. And, even Frank had to admit, his testimony did extreme damage to the argument Frank's defense lawyers had set out to make.

CHAPTER 41

Billie

It wasn't the first time that Billie had sworn on a Bible. But as far as he could remember, Frank Howard's trial *was* the first time that he'd sworn on a Bible and gone on to tell the truth, the whole truth, and nothing but the truth.

"I knew him as 'Mr. John,' " Billie said, while pointing at Frank and looking straight at him.

Frank Howard was dressed in a dark business suit, one that was well cut, with expensive stitching. Billie was wearing a prison jumpsuit that itched and chafed. They looked worlds apart. But Billie was determined to catch Frank's eye. When he did, the look the two men exchanged was significant.

"Let the record show that the witness is pointing to *John* Franklin Howard," the prosecutor told the clerk.

This was the first of several nails that Billie and the prosecutor tried to drive into Frank Howard's coffin.

Methodically, step-by-step, they went through the chronology.

Up in their box, the jurors looked intent and impassive.

"John, Frank, whatever you want to call him. He called me up out of the blue in 2009. I was at home, lying there on the couch. My girlfriend, Stacey, was in the kitchen. And this man said that he'd heard of me, heard I'd be good for the job."

"Did this man specify what that job was?" the prosecutor asked as Billie wriggled around the witness stand.

"Sure he did. He said he wanted to get rid of his wife. Well, do you think I didn't jump up off of that couch?"

"What did you tell the man?"

"I told him I didn't know what he'd heard, or why someone would say that. But if he wanted to meet, we could meet."

"What year was this, to the best of your recollection?"

"This would have been in 2009."

"And did you meet this man 'John'?"

"We met several times," said Billie.

"And what was discussed in the course of these meetings?"

"The ways in which John wanted me to get rid of his wife."

One of the jurors — a middle-aged woman who'd worn sensible shoes and cardigans to every day of the trial — snuck a glance at Nancy. She was sitting on the prosecutor's side of the room, staring straight ahead, betraying no emotion. But at his lawyer's table, Frank shook his head gently from side to side.

"Specifically, if you don't mind," said the prosecutor.

Billie wriggled around in his chair. He glanced over at Nancy, who was still looking straight ahead. He avoided looking at Frank.

"Specifically," Billie said. "With an ax. With a baseball bat. With a gun. He wanted me to kill her while she was at home, with her book club, or something like that. One time he said I could burn her house down. We also talked about carjackings, muggings, cutting the brakes on her car. If she was going out of town for a conference, she could be killed in her hotel. Or she could be killed out in public, like at a restaurant out with her friends. John didn't care too much if other folks got in the way, long as none of us got caught afterward."

The juror in sensible shoes was looking at

Frank now. He was shaking his head more vigorously, whispering to his attorney.

"Wait," the attorney whispered back. "Wait, and he'll give us our opening."

"And did you have any intention of following up on any of these plans that John Frank Howard had made?"

For the first time since he'd taken the stand, Billie looked directly at Frank, who met his gaze and glared at him.

"Hell no, I did not," Billie said.

"So why did you keep talking to Howard?"

"Because every time that we talked, he would give me more money."

"Money for what?"

"For killing his wife is what he said."

"Which you never intended to do?"

"No. But I didn't see that talking about it was some great crime. Not when I never expected to do it. And every time, John would give me more money."

"How much money?"

"Tens of thousands of dollars. Sometimes more. All in all, I'd say he paid out well over a million in cash and another million in bail bonds."

"For something you never came close to doing? Why do you think he'd do that?"

"Objection!" Frank's lawyer called out. "Calls for speculation on the part of the witness."

But the judge let Billie answer the question.

"Well, sir," he said. "Have you ever been of two minds about something important? It seems to me that John was that way about Nancy. If I were to guess, I'd say that he was paying me to listen to him *talk* about killing his wife. The man had money, that much I know. And listening's not much of a crime."

During cross-examination, Frank's defense lawyer was incredulous. In fact, it was as if he'd looked the word *incredulous* up in the dictionary and was working his hardest to live up to the definition. He arched his eyebrows, flapped his arms around, and adopted a mocking tone every time he approached the witness stand where Billie was sitting.

"What you're saying, Mr. Johnson, is that Frank Howard paid you — paid you upwards of two *million* dollars — to listen to him *talk* about killing his wife?" he asked.

"Based on the fact that he kept paying and I kept on listening, I would say yes."

"But killing Nancy Howard was something you never had any intention of doing?"

"No, sir."

"You expect us to believe that?"

"I don't care what you believe. It's the truth."

Billie's really hitting his stride now. His whole life, he'd never understood how easy and simple just telling the truth could be. But now he stopped wriggling around in the witness box. Sitting straight up in his seat, looking right at Frank Howard, he felt righteous and spoke forcefully. It's amazing what the truth can do. Billie wondered why no one had told him about it before.

From here on in, he answered each of the lawyer's questions with as much conviction a simple "No, sir" can carry:

"Isn't the real truth that you contacted Frank Howard and not the other way around?"

"No, sir."

"And that you contacted him because you'd gotten wind of an affair he was having?"

"No, sir."

"And that you intended to blackmail him, in exchange for keeping what you know about his affair to yourself?"

"No, sir."

"And that you did, in fact, blackmail Frank Howard? That you blackmailed him for several years? And that when Frank Howard finally stopped paying, you took revenge on him by shooting his wife?"

"That doesn't even make sense," Billie said, and leaned back in his seat, looking triumphant. But the judge instructed him to answer the lawyer's question.

"No, sir," Billie said. "There was never any talk about blackmail or anything like that."

"Mr. Johnson. Isn't it true that you're in prison now on drug-related charges?"

"Yes, sir, that's true."

"And that by testifying here today, you're hoping to lessen your sentence?"

"No, sir."

"No?"

"I'm here to tell the truth. Whether or not the government sees fit to reduce my sentence, that's up to the government. I'm not a killer. And I haven't been charged with anything having to do with the crime we're talking about today. But what I do know about the Howards is the truth of what happened. That's what I came here to tell you today."

CHAPTER 42

Stacey, Raley, Wall, and Nancy

Frank knew that Billie Earl Johnson had done well on the stand. The blackmail angle had made sense, when Frank's lawyers had presented it to him. But Billie Earl had made it sound ridiculous. Then Billie's girlfriend had taken the stand and backed the things Billie had said right down to the smallest details. The dates she gave matched the ones Billie had given. Her descriptions of meetings with Mr. John synched exactly with the ones her boyfriend had provided.

Stacey admitted it — she knew full well that "Mr. John" was paying Billie to do away with his wife, Nancy Howard. She admitted that she'd enjoyed all the money and all the things she'd bought with it. "It beat working, I'll tell you that much," she said. But backing Billie up again, she said that they'd never planned to go through with the murder.

"This man, Mr. John, never sat right with me," Stacey said. "There's something twisted about him. I told Billie that no good would come out of getting involved in this business. But Billie was never actually going to kill anyone. And Mr. John was just *giving* us money. We weren't stealing. So where was the crime?"

When Frank Howard's defense lawyer asked Stacey about the supposed blackmail plot, she said the same thing Billie had said: "That's ridiculous. That doesn't even make sense!"

Frank's old boss, Richard Raley, took the stand too. Like Billie Earl Johnson, Raley was dressed in an orange jumpsuit. He was in jail on prescription-drug-related charges. But what he told the jury about was the millions of dollars that Frank had stolen from him. The district attorney called an expert witness — a Secret Service agent — to back Raley up, and the agent testified about files and money transfers and all of the spreadsheets on Frank Howard's laptop.

Then Detective Michael Wall took the stand and led the jury through his whole investigation, detail by painstaking detail.

The officer who'd arrived at Nancy's door on the night of the shooting also testified, describing the way she'd looked as he

sprinted up the walkway toward her door —
and the way she had fallen into his arms
once he'd gotten there.

At one point, the beaded, bloodied blouse
that Nancy had worn on the night of the
shooting was shown to the jury. Frank
couldn't help wincing as the prosecutor held
it up. The district attorney played a recording of Nancy's frantic 911 call. He brought
out the 911 operator herself to testify.
Finally, he showed the jury photographs of
the crime scene, with Nancy's blood visible
in all the pictures.

He was like a dog that had gotten ahold
of a really good bone. And Nancy Howard's
own testimony was all the more devastating
for the cool, even tone she delivered it in.

She began by describing the night of the
shooting — her struggle with her assailant,
the cold look in his eyes as she prayed and
begged Jesus to save her.

Then Nancy described the aftermath.

"God spoke to me and said, 'Get up, get
up,' " she told the jury, "and He gave me
the strength to get up."

Nancy had rehearsed her testimony several
times with the prosecutor. She'd rehearsed
it, time and again, in her head. She did not
want to cry on the stand. But it was all she
could do to keep her voice from cracking as

she talked about how it had felt to drag herself out of the garage and through the hallway, and the horror she felt when she looked into the bathroom mirror and saw the "bloody mess" staring back. She described the surgeries she'd had since the shooting — all four of them — and the way her fake eye would fall out of her head, even now, because she lacked the muscles to hold it in place. She talked about the shooting pains she still felt and about losing her senses of taste and smell.

Faith in God and constant prayer pulled her through the experience, she explained.

Finally, Nancy had talked about Frank, who was sitting a few feet away, with a pained look on his face and his hands folded in front of him.

She talked about meeting Frank in his father's church in San Marcos. About how much she had loved his big, lopsided smile. About the way they fell in love and courted, for eleven months, before marrying in that same church. Looking right into his eyes she said, "Frank and I had a great marriage. It wasn't a perfect marriage. But we had a strong relationship."

Was there anything, in the months and weeks that led up to the shooting, that would have led Nancy to believe that Frank could be capable of such a thing?

Looking over at the man who had been her husband, Nancy met Frank's eyes for the first time since the trial had begun. He was smiling at her now — that same old lopsided smile — and she shook her head and said, "Nothing."

CHAPTER 43

The Court

Frank never did testify in his own defense. His lawyers would not risk it, letting him up in the witness stand for the district attorney to savage. They'd staked everything instead on the argument that Billie had blackmailed Frank over his affair, then taken it upon himself to shoot Nancy.

But slowly, systematically, the district attorney's office poked enough holes in that story to sink the *Titanic*. And all the while, the office was building its own mountain of evidence.

There was forensic evidence, gathered at the crime scene. The facts of the shooting were as firmly established as they could have been.

There was the evidence that suggested — all but proved — that Frank Howard had embezzled millions of dollars from Richard Raley. Coupled with Suzanne's testimony about the affair, this established a motive for Frank's actions: Any divorce court judge worth their salt would have discovered the stolen monies immediately, traced them back to Richard Raley, and uncovered Frank's financial crimes.

Frank had gotten in so deep, the DA said, he couldn't have risked a divorce. He could have stayed with Nancy, of course. But Frank wasn't willing to do that. And so, the only alternative, as Frank had seen it, was murder.

Finally, there was the testimony that Billie and Stacey had given — testimony that had been backed up with jailhouse conversations Billie and Frank had had during Billie's various stays in jail. Those jailhouse calls had all been recorded. And on the recordings, which the DA played for the jury, Frank did not sound at all like a man who'd been blackmailed.

"So this thing that we're talking about," Frank would say, over and over again, in the course of these conversations. "When are you going to be able to do it?"

"What you heard there, time and again, had nothing at all to do with blackmail," the prosecutor explained to the jury after playing the last recording. "Clear as day, it was the voice of a man who was contracting another man for a job. In response, Billie Earl Johnson would say, 'Soon, man, soon.' What you're hearing there, time and again, is a man who keeps putting off doing the job. Every one of these conversations backs up everything that Billie Earl Johnson said on the stand."

The sound of Frank implicating himself, directly and repeatedly, set the district attorney up perfectly for his closing argument.

"Ladies and gentlemen," the DA began. "The case before you could not be any more clear. After twenty-eight years of marriage, John Frank Howard hatched a plot to have his wife killed. He hired Billie Earl Johnson, a habitual criminal from East Texas, to kill her. And on August 18, 2012, Nancy Howard was attacked in her home — attacked viciously — by a gunman who shot her in the face and left her for dead."

Frank sat impassively through the district attorney's opening salvo. Nancy's eye followed the DA as he walked, back and forth, in front of the jury box. But like Frank, she betrayed no emotion. The trial had been grueling for her. Testifying against Frank had been the hardest thing she'd ever done, and seeing her own children sitting behind Frank — supporting their father over her —

had been harder still. But the end was in sight now, and Nancy had put her trust in the Lord. Whatever verdict the jury came back with would be a part of His plan.

"Miraculously," the DA continued, "Nancy Howard survived. She will never be the same as she was before the shooting. She's told you, in her own words, about the pain and suffering she's endured already and will continue to endure throughout her life. She described the wounds that will never heal. And along with those wounds, Nancy Howard will have to live the knowledge that her own husband — the father of her three children — stayed with her, under the same roof, for more than two years, while having an affair with another woman *and* planning to have his wife murdered.

"Now, you might ask, why murder? Why didn't John Frank Howard simply obtain a divorce from his wife? Part of the reason has to do with his reluctance to disclose his affair with Suzanne Leontieff. In Carrollton, Howard was seen as a pillar of the community. A churchgoing man who sang in the choir — quite literally, a choirboy.

"He did not want his family, friends, and neighbors to find out about the double life he was leading. And, as you've heard, that double life was doubly complicated, because for several years, Howard had been embezzling funds from his employer, Richard Raley.

"I say 'funds.' But the actual amount that we're talking about is *millions* of dollars. Millions that John Frank Howard used to maintain yet another life — a *triple* life he was leading. As Frank Howard, he was the churchgoing Texan I told you about just a moment ago, as well the lying, philandering husband that Suzanne Leontieff fell in love with in California. But in his *third* life, as 'Mr. John,' he was a man who hatched elaborate fantasies about the ways in which *his own wife* could be murdered. Fantasies that involved baseball bats, house fires, even the murders of innocent bystanders. Fantasies that he fully intended to go through with, and *did* go through with in the end.

"Given this triple life, John Frank Howard felt that he simply could not *afford* a divorce. Not because he had no money. But because a divorce would have laid his finances out for all to see and show the world how he'd gotten that money. If that had happened, we might all still be gathered here today. The only difference would be, we'd be judging this man as a thief, instead of a murderer.

"But John Frank Howard did decide to

205

commit murder and hired Billie Earl Johnson to carry that murder out for him — to shoot Nancy Howard, in cold blood, in her own home, while he was in California, cavorting with his mistress in Lake Tahoe."

Frank remained impassive as the DA went on to catalog the evidence that had been filed against him and summarize the testimony of the witnesses who had been called. Sitting next to his lawyer, he tried to let the DA's words wash past him. They were just words. It would be up to the jury to decide whether or not to believe them. And the last word belonged to Frank's own lawyer.

"Ladies and gentlemen of the jury, you've heard the state make its long, convoluted case against my client," Frank's lawyer said after a short recess the judge had called.

"It's a ridiculous case, a ridiculous story, about a suburban accountant: a family man who grew up in the church and never committed a crime in his life. Suddenly — overnight, the district attorney would have you imagine — this family man becomes a coldhearted criminal. A criminal who spends several years plotting to *destroy* his own family.

"Now, we all know that Frank Howard had an affair. That's not a point of contention today. That's not what Frank Howard's on trial for. Like the rest of us, he's made mistakes. Like all of us, he's a sinner. But even the district attorney knows there's no logical connection between Frank Howard's love affair and the terrible thing that happened to Nancy Howard. The district attorney knows there's not one shred of physical evidence that links Frank Howard to his wife's shooting. He knows that Frank Howard was in California on the night that shooting took place. In fact, he's got so little to go on, he's had to trot *actual* criminals out to do what criminals tend to do — lie. And those lies are the basis of the state's entire case against Frank Howard."

Frank had not turned his head once during the DA's closing argument. He did not turn it now. But suddenly he could feel Nancy's gaze on the back of his neck and imagined her, sitting a few feet away, judging him.

For many years now, Frank had thought that Nancy was weak — not much more than a weight around his ankles. But Nancy's testimony had changed his mind. Seeing how calm she'd remained up on the stand. How put together she'd seemed as she walked the jury through the sordid details of the shooting. Now, as his lawyer addressed the jury, Frank looked inside of himself for the faith he'd seen Nancy exhibit and found himself praying for the same kind of strength.

"You heard from Billie Earl Johnson, a drug addict who's spent his whole life in and out of prison and only testified here in exchange for a reduced sentence," Frank's lawyer was saying. "You've heard from another drug addict, Richard Raley, who told improbable stories about millions of dollars that Frank Howard stole. Somehow, the district attorney would have you believe that there's a link between this money that you heard Raley talking about and the shooting of Nancy Howard. What I want to ask you now is, how in the world does that make any sense?

"What I want to ask is, why would a man who's already had *one* divorce decide to murder his *second* wife, instead of simply divorcing her too? A family man, like Frank Howard, who'd been in his marriage for going on thirty years. A man who had three loving children — all of whom testified on his behalf. A man who slipped in his marriage, as some of us do. But who *loved* his wife, stuck by her side, and saw her through the terrible aftermath of the shooting? The reason Frank Howard didn't obtain a divorce from his wife is that he *didn't want to divorce her.*

"Now, we'll get down to details in a moment. This is an extremely convoluted case, the case that the government's making. It's so convoluted, it might take us a while to untangle. So before we do, let's stop for a moment and look at the much simpler facts, insofar as they pertain to the actual circumstances leading up to the shooting of Nancy Howard."

As his lawyer laid out the facts, Frank was impressed with his delivery. No longer praying, he hung on to the lawyer's every word. And as he looked up, Frank saw that the men and the women gathered there to sit in judgment of him were doing the same.

"Ladies and gentlemen, before we get to the details, which will exonerate my client once and for all, let me ask you: Which story is more believable? Which one's in line with everything you've heard about the characters involved? And, because in my experience as a criminal attorney, simple explanations are the ones that always tend to be right, let me ask you one more thing: Which story is *simpler*?"

It's a strong argument, Frank thought when his lawyer was done. Strong and simple, like the lawyer had said. The district attorney had talked about double lives, triple lives. But who'd ever heard of somebody leading a *triple* life? Just a few years earlier, Frank himself wouldn't have believed it to be possible. Would he have been capable of an affair? Of course. With Frank, women were always a weakness. But would he have been capable of embezzlement on a grand scale? Of consorting with criminals? Ultimately, would he have been capable of murder?

If the old Frank Howard had been there, in the jury box, he would not have believed any of it. The old Frank Howard would never have voted to convict.

But the old Frank Howard was gone. And when the Frank Howard that remained scanned the jurors' faces, not one of them met his eye. The middle-aged juror in sensible shoes was looking down at her lap. The middle-aged man who'd worn a three-piece suit to every day of the trial was glancing back and forth between Frank's lawyer and the thick notepad that he'd been scribbling in. The girl who taken time off from her job as a dental hygienist (she had the same job as Frank's mistress, Suzanne, and had taken a special interest in Suzanne's testimony) stared off to the side, as if something more interesting were happening in the courtroom's far corner.

Frank tried once more to catch their eye. Once again, none of them — not even the alternate jurors — would meet his gaze. And as Frank's lawyer wrapped up his concluding argument, and the jurors filed, slowly, out of the courtroom, Frank thought that he saw a look of firm, fixed determination on each of the juror's faces.

In Frank's estimation, none of this was a good sign.

CHAPTER 44

Frank

The jury deliberated for just two hours before coming back with its verdict:

Guilty.

Two hours! Frank's lawyer had told him that it would take the jurors at least a few hours to simply go over the charges. What this meant, then, was that they hadn't had to deliberate at all.

Nancy's expression was impossible to read. She sat stock-still, with her hands in her lap, staring straight ahead into the distance. But Frank's children, who had sat behind their father throughout the trial and not on Nancy's side of the courtroom, were visibly angry. They stormed out of the courtroom without saying a word to their mother.

Nancy knew they would blame her for not having done more to help Frank beat the charges. But what more could she have done? Every word Nancy had said on the stand was true. It had been a fair trial. Frank's lawyers had done the best they could have done, given what they'd had to work with. And, in the end, the jury had made up its mind. There would be an appeal, Nancy was sure. Another trial. She would see Frank again. But as she looked over at him in the courtroom, Nancy saw something else. Her husband, Frank Howard, was gone. The man sitting in his chair now was someone else — a stranger.

It was *John* Howard that Nancy was looking at now.

Mr. John.

Frank was almost relieved.

He had survived the worst thing he feared could have happened to him. All of the witnesses, there on parade, were like walk-ons in the story of his life. Each time one of them told just a bit of the truth — and really, Frank knew, it was only his lawyers who'd lied — it was the lifting of a burden that Frank had been carrying for years. If he'd been younger, he would have been better at juggling all his affairs: his love affairs, and all the money he'd stolen from Raley. But Frank was older and slower now, and once he'd dropped that first ball he'd been juggling, his world had crashed down all around him. For a long time before the shooting, he'd been frantic. So anxious, for so long, he'd gotten used to it. He had not allowed himself to *feel* the anxiety. But it was there all along, and it got so much worse in the aftermath of the shooting. Now, as he sat in the rubble and ruins of his own life, Frank felt still and at peace. It was a feeling he had not known in years. There was nothing to hide now. No more trouble that he could get himself into. Nothing to fear.

Frank stayed in that state for some hours after the verdict, and the days that followed were full of calm. Even walking back into the courtroom for sentencing didn't alarm him.

"Life" was a sentence Frank Howard had been serving all along.

CHAPTER 45

Nancy

The house on Bluebonnet Way was so quiet now. Nancy still prayed, every day, that the time would come when her children forgave her.

Hearing about Frank's infidelity had shocked Ashley, Jed, and Brianna — even shattered them. If they didn't know their own father, what *did* they know? What could they be sure of?

The answer turned out to be simple: The children were sure of Frank's innocence. They *had* to be, because the world in which Frank was guilty was a world that no longer made sense.

She was proud of them, even, for being so loyal to their father, as misguided as that loyalty had turned out to be. But she was also conflicted. Wasn't being on Frank's side the same as wishing that Nancy, their mother, was dead? That was what Frank had wanted, after all. And though Frank had failed, there *was* a sense in which he had succeeded. He'd wanted to break Nancy's family apart, and he'd done that. He'd wanted to take her away from the children, and he had done that too. The way things turned out might not have been the end result Frank was after, but from Nancy's perspective, it amounted to much the same thing.

It was all so terribly unfair.

Still, Nancy was glad to be alive. She had her faith, and the hatred she did feel for Frank, in her weaker moments, had less to do with his actions in and of themselves than with the ways in which those actions had tested her beliefs. The long nights that had followed the shooting had taken Nancy down some of the darkest paths that she had ever been on. It was the only time in her life that she'd asked Jesus questions and found herself doubting the answers. But she'd come out into the light at the end of that tunnel, and she tried hard not to hate, to forgive, and be grateful for the good things in her life:

Her church. Her faith. The friends who had stuck by her.

The family would recover, she thought. Just as Nancy herself had recovered. God's grace was infinite, and Nancy prayed more for it now than she ever had before the shooting. If anything, Nancy knew the long trial that she'd gone through had only *strengthened* her faith. That was just one of the miracles she had been blessed to receive.

Now, in church and at home, Nancy ended her prayers by thanking Jesus for her second chance and by asking God to bring her children home to her.

Then, soberly, she would pray for the salvation of John Frank Howard's soul.

Mother of All Murders

JAMES PATTERSON
WITH CHRISTOPHER CHARLES

CHAPTER 1

Aleah has read the same page of her history text a half-dozen times and still can't remember the name of Henry VIII's first wife. It's impossible to concentrate with her parents arguing on the other side of a paper-thin wall — especially when they're arguing about her.

"We need that money for Aleah's college," her mother says.

"Really?" her father says. "With her grades, she'll be lucky if she graduates."

"So your solution is to put a down payment on a brand-new SUV?"

"I'm not solving anything. There's nothing to solve. She's getting a job and that's it."

Aleah slams the book shut, gets out of bed, sits at her desk, and taps the spacebar on her computer. The monitor lights up. She refreshes her Facebook page, clicks on the messages icon, then types in the name of her best friend and neighbor: Gypsy Rose.

"Hey, Gypsy," she writes, "I thought you were going to send me pictures of your 'Secret Sam'!!!"

She hits Return, waits.

Her parents keep at it. She hears them moving back and forth between the kitchen and living room, screaming at each other as if they're standing a football field apart.

"What kind of job will she get with no education?" her mother asks.

"She has as much education as you or me."

"That's my point."

Aleah hits the Refresh button. She can see that Gypsy has read her message, but still no response.

"PHOTOS PLEASE!!!" Aleah types. "You wouldn't believe the night I'm having."

She stares at the screen, hears her father say: "Some people aren't cut out for college. There's no shame in it."

The computer makes a pinging sound, and a red "1" appears at the top of the page. Aleah clicks as fast as she can. Instead of photos, she finds a message from Gypsy:

"THAT BITCH IS DEAD."

Aleah pushes back in her chair, feels her pulse quicken. She's never heard Gypsy say so much as "damn."

She hits Refresh again, hoping for a punch line. After a long beat, she yells, "MOM!!!"

Twenty minutes later, she's sitting at the front window with her mother, watching two cops approach Gypsy's front door. The shorter of the two rings the bell, then presses his face to the side glass panel. The taller one shakes his head, knocks with his baton, and seems startled when the door, unlocked, swings open a few inches. They look at each other, then step inside.

"Police," Officer Weir, the shorter one, calls. "Anyone home?"

Officer Crace, Weir's partner, switches on an overhead light. They are standing in an L-shaped living/dining area. The space is crowded with oversized furniture and a robust collection of medical supplies: expensive-looking wheelchairs line the back wall; the long dining table is nearly covered in pill bottles and syringes; a series of shelves house braces and casts shaped like every body part a person might injure.

"This some kind of clinic?" Crace asks.

"Just a residence," Weir says.

"Hello," Crace calls. "It's the police."

No answer.

"What did the message say again?" Crace asks.

"That bitch is dead."

"And it was the daughter who sent it?"

"Yeah."

"Any info on her?"

"The 911 caller said she's a shut-in. Sick since the day she was born."

Crace points to the row of wheelchairs.

"So I guess those are hers?" he asks.

"Looks like she's got one for every day of the week."

"We know anything about the mother?"

"Name's Dee Dee Blancharde. Single mom. Used to be some kind of medical assistant. Now she just takes care of her gimpy kid."

"All right," Crace says. "Let's have a look around."

They start down a narrow hallway off the dining area. Crace takes the first door on the right: Dee Dee's bedroom. The room is pitch dark. He switches on the overhead. A blackout shade covers the only window. An unmade king-size bed with a noticeable sag in the middle takes up most of the room. The air smells of vapor rubs and menthol. There's a thick, well-worn medical encyclopedia on the nightstand.

His partner calls for him from the next

room: "Crace, get in here. You've got to see this."

He finds Weir standing at the center of what looks like a dollhouse bedroom built to human scale: yellow walls with rose-patterned wallpaper trim, a canopy bed with hospital-style rails, pristine shag area rugs, a white dresser with gold handles and a heart-shaped mirror, a matching white desk to house Gypsy's computer. The wall above the computer is plastered with intricate, detailed drawings that might have been ripped from a fantasy video game — pages and pages of monsters and dragons and women in tight-fitting armor wielding swords.

"It's just a bedroom," Crace says.

"Yeah, but there's something creepy about it," Weir says. "It doesn't fit with the rest of the house. It's like walking into a shrine or one of those museum recreations. Everything's a little too perfect."

"If you say so."

Weir starts for the door, stumbles over an object buried in one of the shag rugs.

"What's this?" he asks.

He kneels down, finds a beige inhaler with a chewed up mouthpiece.

"Jesus," Crace says. "Is anything *not* wrong with this girl?"

They move back through the dining area and into the kitchen. And that's where they find her: Dee Dee Blancharde sprawled on the linoleum floor, her plain white shift soaked in blood.

CHAPTER 2

"Good God, how much do think she weighs?" Detective Brian Slater asks. "Gotta be three fifty, easy."

"Still counts as one victim," his new partner, Detective Emily Draper, says.

They're staring down at Dee Dee Blancharde's body while a CSI team moves through the house behind them. Slater counts four distinct stab wounds. He pulls at the cuff of one of his latex gloves and lets go, like snapping a rubber band against his wrist.

"Any sign of the knife?" he asks a passing crime tech.

"Nothing yet, boss," the man says.

"All right," Slater tells Draper. "Let's take a little tour."

They start with the pill bottles and syringes on the dining room table. Draper reads the labels out loud: "Eteplirsen, Mexitil, Prednisone, Sprycel, Clafen, Zolpidem,

Klonopin . . ."

"All for the daughter?" Slater asks.

"Looks that way."

"You'd think the meds alone would kill her," Slater says. "Let's get the names of her docs."

Draper takes out her phone, starts snapping pictures of the bottles. Slater turns his attention to the wheelchairs. There's a column of folded manuals stacked five high. There's a forest-green motorized recliner with a joystick for steering, a bright-red scooter with a wire basket in front that makes Slater think of *The Wizard of Oz.*

"That's a hell of a collection," he says. "I can't see how a person would need more than one."

"Girls like to accessorize," Draper says.

"Those are some pricey accessories."

"Depends who paid for them. Maybe they had some kind of mega insurance."

"Yeah, maybe," Slater says.

They move on to Dee Dee's room. Slater begins rifling through the dresser drawers, hoping to turn up a diary. Draper digs through the closet, beginning with the jam-packed clothes rack. Among the colorful striped shirts, smocks, and overalls, she finds a stash of costumes: a purple fleece bathrobe with a *Star Trek* delta shield sewn onto the left breast pocket; a pair of moss-green fairy wings dangling from a wooden hanger; a plus-size silver jumpsuit with a thick black belt and what looks like a computer screen painted across the chest.

"A little old for trick or treating," Draper says under her breath.

She kneels, pushes aside a heap of shoes and boots, finds a knee-high safe with an electronic lock. The door is wide open.

"Hey, Brian," she calls. "I've got something here."

Slater crouches behind her, whistles.

"Nice find for a rookie," he says.

"Or do you mean for a woman?"

"Do me a favor," Slater grins. "Wait till I say something offensive before you get offended."

Draper reaches into the safe, pulls out a small spiral pad, flips through the pages.

"It's a ledger," she says.

Slater reads over her shoulder. The most recent page lists, in bright red block letters, payments from a half-dozen charitable foundations, among them the Springfield Leukemia Society, the Knights of Columbus, and the First Methodist Church of Springfield. The total comes to just over $4,000.

Draper runs her hand across the floor of

the safe, comes away with a single rubber band.

"This is what's left of the money," she says.

Slater stands, smooths out a crease in his pants.

"Curiouser and curiouser," he says. "Whoever killed her knew the combination."

"Or forced it out of her."

Slater gives a skeptical shrug.

"Could be," he says. "But there are no signs of torture. No signs of any struggle outside the kitchen."

They get a crime scene tech to dust the safe and bag the ledger, then move on to Gypsy's dollhouse bedroom.

"Not sure I've seen a canopy hospital bed before," Draper says. "Is it possible to be crippled *and* spoiled?"

Slater points to the desk: "We'll need to get forensics on that computer."

Draper goes through the gold-handled drawers while Slater studies Gypsy's drawings. He is taken by the exaggerated yet controlled lines, the way a wolf with wings looks like it might fly off the page, the way a gargoyle's fangs blossom into thorny roses. *The girl has talent,* he thinks. *Even if fantasy is so much bunk.*

He spots a drawing that isn't like the others: a simple headstone, rounded at the edges, with nothing but clouds in the background. There's an engraving at the top of the stone: RIP GYPSY ROSE BLANCHARDE.

"What do you make of this?" he asks Draper.

She moves closer, stands on tiptoes.

"Maybe those are the two things she wants most," Draper says.

"Which two things?"

"Rest and peace."

Draper and Slater stand outside the Blancharde home, Slater smoking an unfiltered cigarette, Draper sipping cold coffee from a paper cup.

"Hell of a duo," Slater says, "for such a quiet street."

"These little suburban houses pack a lot of drama," Draper says. "Nobody really knows what goes on inside them."

Slater grins.

"That's deep," he says, blowing out a long stream of smoke. Draper punches his arm.

"So what do you think?" Slater asks. "Someone stabs the mother and makes off with the girl?"

"Looks like it."

"The father, maybe?"

"I had one of the uniforms check on him.

He's down in Louisiana with an airtight alibi. Seems he's been out of the picture for years."

"Maybe Dee Dee Blancharde had a beau," Slater says. "No forced entry. The code to the safe. Had to be someone they knew."

"But why take the girl?"

Slater shrugs.

"People have every kind of fetish," he says.

"OK, but why take the girl and not her meds? Anyone who knew them had to know how sick she was."

Slater looks up and down street as though he expects to see Gypsy Rose turn a corner on one of her motorized wheelchairs.

"Maybe that's the fetish," he says. "Maybe whoever took her wants to watch her die."

CHAPTER 3

Pastor Mike steps to a small podium at the center of the lawn and signals for everyone to gather round. Dee Dee Blancharde stands beside him, her fingers gripping the backrest of Gypsy's Lightweight Cruiser Deluxe. Gypsy, in her frilly white hat with the pompoms dangling off the sides, manages to look happy and carefree despite the wheelchair, despite the oxygen tank and the tubes running from her nose.

"Come now," Pastor Mike shouts. "It's time to begin."

Neighbors step away from the folding-table buffet to join the circle of reporters, photographers, and churchgoers.

"This is truly a blessed day," Pastor Mike says, raising his cupped hands skyward. "We have here two people whose long and harrowing journey ought to inspire us all. Dee Dee Blancharde and her daughter, Gypsy Rose, have persevered through every shape and form of adversity. But the daughter, plagued by illness, has been anything but a burden to her loving mother. With a strength that smacks of God's love, Dee Dee Blancharde has outsmarted and outlasted obstacles of biblical proportions. They were driven from their Louisiana home by Katrina's wrath, the daughter sick with cancer and muscular dystrophy, the mother exhausted beyond measure, and now, finally, they have found a soft place to land. They have found this place, this house standing here behind me which we at Springfield Methodist could not be more pleased to have built for them, complete with all the modifications necessary for a girl in Gypsy Rose's condition. Please join me in welcoming them into our community."

There's a round of applause as the pastor steps aside and Anne-Marie Burrell of Channel 4's *Mornings with Anne-Marie* takes his place. She's in her early forties, pretty in a regional-television way, though Dee Dee wonders what kind of flaws all that makeup is hiding. Cameramen disperse around her, two on either side and one kneeling in front of the podium.

"Good morning, everyone," she starts, stretching her flawless smile as wide as it will go.

"Good morning, Anne-Marie," the small crowd returns.

Dee Dee looks out at the strangers gathered on her lawn, thinks: *people will do anything to catch a glimpse of themselves on the idiot box.*

"Thank you all for coming," Anne-Marie continues. "This is, as Pastor Mike said, a blessed day. Like you, I'm here to honor and celebrate the work Pastor Mike and his congregation have done . . ."

She gestures to the small white house with the long, trellised wheelchair ramp.

"It's generous and exceptional acts like this one that make a community. As I always say, if we can't live for each other, then why live at all?"

Dee Dee forces a smile, but she feels embarrassed — not because she'll be seen as some kind of parasite, but because people don't understand how hard she's worked: raising a disabled child alone is just one of her full-time jobs; the other is soliciting help.

"All right, then," Anne-Marie says. "Without further ado, let's see the inside."

The three-man camera crew follows close behind as Dee Dee wheels Gypsy up the ramp. Anne-Marie takes the lead, playing tour guide.

"Notice how the ramp and the floors are

made of the same light pine," she says as they enter the home. "It's like the inside is a continuation of the outside."

Dee Dee stares down at the floorboards, eyes wide, hands covering her cheeks.

"Goodness, how they shine," she says. "You can almost see yourself in them. Isn't that right, Gypsy?"

She nudges her daughter's shoulder.

"They're so fancy," Gypsy observes, tugging at one of her hat's pompoms. "I feel like a movie star."

"The furniture is all top of the line," Anne-Marie says with a sweeping, Vanna White gesture. "Donated by the Springfield Emporium's downtown location."

Dee Dee lets her jaw drop as she takes in the long mahogany dining table, the wraparound sectional facing a large-screen TV.

"Magnificent," she says, though in truth the space feels cramped, and she is just now noticing the lack of natural light.

"Magnificent," Gypsy parrots.

Anne-Marie leads them into the kitchen (stainless steel can't disguise the matchbox size), then back through the dining area and down the hall (barely wide enough for Gypsy's wheelchair or Dee Dee's girth — they might have thought about that) leading to the bedrooms and bathroom. The cameramen follow like hungry puppies. It's clear from the way they dress — baggy jeans, patchy facial hair, T-shirts advertising their friends' rock bands — that they have no intention of ever standing in front of the camera.

"Feel the mattress," Anne-Marie instructs Dee Dee as they take their positions on opposite sides of the king-size bed. "It's memory foam. I have the same model *chez moi.* Trust me, you'll sleep better than you ever have before."

Dee Dee leans forward, presses down with both hands, watches the foam rise up around her fingers.

"Oh, I'll be hitting the hay early tonight," she says.

Anne-Marie smiles, gives a little wink as if to say: *You're doing great!* Dee Dee looks the room over, thinks: *Why'd they put the damn window where all you can see is the neighbor's rotting fence?*

They move to Gypsy's room, the home's crown jewel. It has to be the crown jewel, of course, because Gypsy is the real charity case here. Anne-Marie's audience will want to believe that a canopy bed and pretty wallpaper make up for a lifetime of paralysis and eye surgeries and needles and crumbling teeth and brittle bones from a diet that's more pills than food.

Poor girl, Dee Dee thinks.

They've reached the climax of the tour, and anything less than pure joy will mean that they never see another dime from Springfield Methodist. This time, Dee Dee asks the question herself. She steps in front of her daughter, crouches a little, puts on a wide smile.

"So," she says, "what do you think?"

Gypsy does not disappoint. She looks up and, through a grin that shows more gum than teeth, says:

"I must be the luckiest girl in the world."

The cameramen hold her in frame, then turn to Anne-Marie, who is absolutely glowing with compassion.

CHAPTER 4

The *Mornings with Anne-Marie* crew has transformed Dee Dee's living room into a TV studio. There are bright lights on tripods pointed at Dee Dee and Gypsy where they sit side by side on the extra-long couch. A makeup artist gives them both a quick touch-up before the cameras resume rolling.

Anne-Marie sits across from them in an armchair that wasn't there before and isn't theirs to keep. Her skin is barely visible through all the blush and powder, and she's hitched her skirt to show more leg. Dee Dee wonders why the bother: it's not like she's competing with the cast of *Charlie's Angels.*

A crew member steps forward and yells "Action," just like in the movies.

"I'm back with Dee Dee Blancharde and her daughter, Gypsy Rose," Anne-Marie tells the camera before turning to her guests. "If you wouldn't mind, I'd like to give my viewers a bit more of your background. Your journey has been a harrowing one, but at its core it's also an uplifting story that speaks to human love and resilience."

Journey . . . harrowing . . . uplifting . . . Dee Dee checks off the clichés in her head. Not that she minds: she's learned how to make clichés work to her benefit. More importantly, she's learned to make them work to her daughter's benefit.

"Tell me," Anne-Marie says, "when did you first learn that Gypsy was ill?"

Dee Dee, who approved the questions in advance, tilts her head as though searching her memory for the exact moment it all began.

"When she was still a baby, I noticed she couldn't hardly breathe and took her straight to the emergency."

"This was in New Orleans?"

"Yes ma'am. Everything was in New Orleans till Katrina hit."

"So it started with —"

"Sleep apnea," Dee Dee says. "I knew a little something about it 'cause I'd started training to be a nurses' aide."

As if to confirm the diagnosis, Gypsy adjusts the tubes in her nose.

"From there," Dee Dee says, "it just all went downhill at a million miles an hour.

She'd get one ear infection after another after another. By the time she was six months it was clear her eyes were no good. I'd shake a rattle right in front of her and she wouldn't even look at it. She wasn't a year yet when she had her first eye surgery."

"As a mother," Anne-Marie says, "I can only imagine how frightening that must have been."

A cameraman points his lens at Gypsy, then quickly turns away. Her eyes are drifting around the room and she's fiddling with a clump of fabric on her hat. It isn't that she's stopped listening: it's that she's heard this all before and is waiting for her cue to tune back in.

"I was all-the-way terrified," Dee Dee says. "And from there things just kept getting scarier and scarier. She started having seizures. About one a month, maybe more if she had any in her sleep when I couldn't be watching. Her little body'd start shaking like she was about to speak in tongues. That's when I knew she had epilepsy."

"Epilepsy?" Anne-Marie asks, resting her crossed forearms on one knee and doing her best to look sympathetic.

"Oh, yes," Dee Dee says. "But that wasn't hardly the worst of it. By the time she was eighteen months and still couldn't so much as stand on her own two feet, I figured for sure there had to be something wrong deep in her bones. They did every test on her you could imagine. The tests themselves was the worst part. Gypsy wouldn't cry, she'd wail. One time I just lost it. I screamed, *You're killing my baby.* A nurse brought me to the cafeteria and bought me a chamomile tea to calm my nerves."

"You must have been beside yourself," Anne-Marie says. "Any mother would be."

"I wished it was me lying in a hospital bed, getting poked and prodded and having all kinds of dye injected into my veins. I'd have given anything to trade places with her."

She takes a handkerchief from her pocket and dabs beneath her eyes. The cameras zoom in.

"Please, take a minute," Anne-Marie says.

Gypsy places a hand on her mother's knee.

"I'm all right," Dee Dee says. "It's just . . . we're coming to a part I don't much like to remember."

Anne-Marie tunes her voice to its most somber pitch: "The test results?" she asks.

Dee Dee nods.

"Muscular dystrophy. I was prepared for that. It made sense with the way she couldn't walk right. But then they came back with leukemia. That melted me. I thought it was a death sentence. I never would've believed I'd be sitting here with my baby all these years later."

She leans over, gives Gypsy a little peck on the cheek. Gypsy bats her eyes.

"I have to ask," Anne-Marie says. "How is it possible for one child to suffer so many afflictions?"

"That was the question I kept asking," Dee Dee says. "I can't explain it the way the doctors did, but Gypsy has what they call a chromosomal defect. That's the source of everything she's got wrong with her."

She runs the handkerchief over her face: those TV lights are hot like the sun. She's in the zone now. She's almost forgotten who she's telling her story to and why. As if Anne-Marie weren't there. As if the cameras weren't there. As if there was no one in the world besides her and Gypsy.

CHAPTER 5

"Did you have any help during this period?" Anne-Marie asks.

They are back and freshly powdered after a final commercial break.

"The government helped us a bunch," Dee Dee says. "I didn't hardly pay a dime to any doctor or hospital."

"What about emotional support?"

"Who was gonna look out for me?" Dee Dee asks. "Except for Gypsy, I was on my own. It's just been me and her from the very beginning. Her daddy don't even know her name. And to tell you the truth, I've just about forgot his."

"But you were married?"

"For a heartbeat. I wasn't seventeen yet when he got me pregnant." She almost said *knocked me up.* "He thought he'd do the right thing, but the marriage didn't last half as long as the pregnancy. Kids having kids, I guess. Not that I regret a thing. Gypsy is my world."

"You're lucky to have such a devoted mother," Anne-Marie tells Gypsy.

Gypsy sits up straight, comes suddenly alive.

"I don't hardly look on her like she's my mom. It's like we're the same person. I think something and she says it. We're two peas in a pod."

It's the first time she's spoken at length, and her voice — high pitched and bursting with energy, like a young child's — startles Anne-Marie.

"A brand-new pod, as of today," she points out.

"We're truly blessed," Dee Dee says. "The people of Springfield have been so good to us. I just hope I can repay them somehow."

"I don't think you have to worry about that," Anne-Marie says. "Speaking of Springfield, what brought you here? It's a big country, and from what I understand, you don't have any roots in Missouri."

Dee Dee detects a hint of accusation in her tone, as though Anne-Marie's real question is: "How exactly did you come to prey on our community?" *Careful how you answer,* Dee Dee tells herself.

"Katrina darn near killed us," she starts. "It destroyed our home. Washed it off the face of the earth. Destroyed Gypsy's medical records, too. We wound up in a shelter with no money and just enough medicine to keep Gypsy alive. It was a female doctor at the shelter who suggested a clinic in Springfield. She grew up here, I think. She's the one put me in touch with Pastor Mike. She arranged it all. I owe her everything. Sometimes I break down thinking on just how much I owe."

"But isn't it natural," Anne-Marie asks, "for people whose lives are relatively easy to want to help people whose lives are hard?"

And now the Oprah moment, Dee Dee thinks. *Free counseling, if you call spilling your guts on television free.*

"Well," she says, "if things was reversed, I'd like to think I'd do the same."

"You would, Mama," Gypsy says, resting her head on her mother's shoulder. "I know you would. I know better than anyone."

That night, neighbor after neighbor drops by. They come bearing Crock-Pots and casseroles full of piping hot food. A little later, the dessert brigade shows up with ambrosia, German layer cake, pies of every kind. Dee Dee and Gypsy live at the end of a cul-de-sac in a small neighborhood: some of these smiling, well-dressed women must have driven a long way to catch a glimpse of the new local attraction.

By eight thirty, the doorbell has quit ringing. Dee Dee sets two plates at the end of a table loaded with more food than she could eat in a month.

"Our first meal in our new home," she says, wheeling Gypsy over.

"It all smells so good," Gypsy says.

Dee Dee ties a bib around her daughter's neck.

"Here's hoping none of it is poisoned," she says.

"Mama!" Gypsy scolds. "People are being real good to us. You know they are."

"Only takes one," Dee Dee says. "Might be some kind soul wants to put us out of our misery."

She walks into the kitchen, comes back carrying a large bowl, a can of Pediasure, and a banana. She fills her bowl to the brim with lamb stew, places the can and banana in front of Gypsy.

"But Mama," Gypsy says, "my stomach's good tonight."

"And we want to make sure it stays that way."

"Just this once? If this ain't a special occasion, then what is?"

"Let's see you keep that down first."

"But Mama —"

"That's enough now."

Dee Dee drops her hands flat on the table, gives Gypsy a look that says negotiations are done for the evening.

"Sorry, Mama," Gypsy says. "You want me to say grace now?"

"I think God's answered enough prayers for one day, don't you?"

Dee Dee stabs a piece of lamb with her fork, plunges it deeper into the gravy, then pulls it out and swallows it whole. Gypsy takes a sip of her chocolate drink. It tastes like chemicals and coats the roof of her mouth with what feels like chalk. She eyes the lemon meringue pie sitting just out of reach, suppresses a little whimper.

CHAPTER 6

Dr. Dan Ryan's office is large and modern, the walls decorated with posters listing the signs and symptoms of a dozen different diseases. Dee Dee reads them over while she and Gypsy wait for the doctor to make his entrance. Psoriasis causes joint pain. Hypoglycemia causes excessive sweating. Dee Dee takes careful mental notes.

"Well, I'll be," she says. "No matter how long you live, you just keep learning."

Gypsy, who is busy tearing a callus from her right palm, refuses to quit pouting.

"I still don't see why I've gotta wear this dumb bandana," she says.

"There's nothing dumb about it," Dee Dee says. "Light blue compliments your eyes. Besides which, you can't go around in that silly hat every day of your life. A doctor's office is a dignified place."

Gypsy starts to protest, stops when the door swings open and Dr. Ryan steps into the room.

"How are we doing today?" he asks.

"Good," Gypsy tells him.

"Oh, you'd say 'good' if you were drowning in quicksand," Dee Dee says. "Let the doctor decide how you are."

Dr. Ryan grins at Gypsy.

"Well, good isn't a bad place to start," he says. "What brings you here today?"

There's something about him that Dee Dee instantly dislikes. She doesn't approve of his grass-stained tennis shoes, the gel in his spiky white hair, the metallic-smelling aftershave. A doctor should be plain, neutral. You shouldn't notice anything about him at all.

"Oh, you're going to earn your money today, Doctor," she says.

She lists Gypsy's ailments, from asthma to cancer, eczema to paralysis. Dr. Ryan's eyes grow wide. Dee Dee wonders if he saw yesterday's episode of *Mornings with Anne-Marie*.

"Well, let's have a look at you," Dr. Ryan says, adjusting his stethoscope. He listens to Gypsy's heart, looks inside her ears, sticks a tongue depressor in her mouth and asks her to cough, does a double-take when he sees her blackened, crumbling teeth. He has her push against his hands with all of her might, turn her head as far to the left and right as it will go.

"Any of that hurt?" he asks.

"Nope," Gypsy says.

"She's been in pain her whole life, Doctor," Dee Dee says. "She wouldn't know the difference."

Dr. Ryan jots a few notes on Gypsy's chart.

"She has quite a history," he tells Dee Dee. "We'll need her full medical records."

He must not watch Anne-Marie, Dee Dee thinks. *Probably out getting in an early round of golf.*

"That's the problem, Doctor. We're transplants. Maybe 'refugees' is the word. All her records got washed away in Katrina. But I got every detail stored up here," Dee Dee says, tapping her skull. "Anything you want to know, just ask."

"Sounds like the two of you have been through the ringer," Dr. Ryan says.

"And we're stronger for it, God willing."

Dr. Ryan runs the backs of his fingers over his clean-shaven cheeks while he considers his next step.

"Do me a favor, Gypsy. Stand up for me."

"But I told you, Doctor," Dee Dee says, "the girl's paralyzed."

"Still, I'd like to see her try."

251

Dee Dee moves to Gypsy's side, places a hand under her elbow.

"No, no," Dr. Ryan says. "I need her to do it alone."

"My girl hasn't stood on her own two feet since . . . since forever."

Ryan crouches in front of Gypsy, pats her arm.

"Why don't you try it for me?" he says. "I'll catch you if you fall."

"All right," Gypsy says. "I'll try."

She's trembling, biting at her lower lip.

"Good girl," Dr. Ryan says.

He positions himself behind the wheel-chair. Gypsy pushes on the armrests, rises without so much as wobbling. Dee Dee, tears in her eyes, lets out a little gasp.

"Excellent," Dr. Ryan says. "Now, can you turn so that you're facing me?"

Gypsy looks at her mother. Dee Dee appears panic-stricken, as though her daughter is navigating a ledge thirty stories above street level.

"Go ahead, now," Dr. Ryan says. "Give it a shot."

Gypsy pivots one foot, then the next. Her slippers make a dragging sound on the floor as she shuffles 180 degrees. Her movements are stiff, unnatural, but she has little difficulty reversing direction. Dr. Ryan flashes a big smile.

"Your legs look strong to me," he says. "I don't see any reason why you can't walk."

"I told you why," Dee Dee says. "I told you plenty of reasons why. Don't forget, I been there since the beginning. I been through it all with her."

Gypsy sits back down, awkwardly, looking as though she's been reprimanded. Dr. Ryan crosses his arms, leans back against a counter lined with canisters of cotton swabs and syringes.

"I tell you what, Gypsy," he says. "We're going to try a brand-new test. You aren't afraid of the dark, are you?"

"No sir."

"What kind of test?" Dee Dee asks, suspicious.

"It's totally safe, and totally painless," Dr. Ryan says, speaking directly to Gypsy. "We use it to check for nerve damage. All you have to do is keep your eyes on a small circle of light while it moves around a dark room. Any time the light vanishes, you clap your hands. Simple, right?"

Gypsy nods.

"I guess that's okay," Dee Dee says, trying to hide her scowl.

"Very good," Dr. Ryan says. "I just need to move you to the testing room at the end of the hall."

Dee Dee stands, picks up her purse.

"I'm sorry, Ms. Blancharde," Dr. Ryan says. "You'll have to sit this one out."

Her stare stops just short of a snarl.

"I never sat out a thing in my girl's life."

"I'm sorry, but the testing room will only accommodate a single patient. We won't be long."

Dee Dee debates whether or not to walk out right then and there, but Gypsy, who has taken a liking to this new doctor, says: "Don't worry about me, Mama. I'll be fine."

Before Dee Dee can respond, Dr. Ryan is holding the door open, and Gypsy is wheeling herself into the hall.

CHAPTER 7

The testing room looks to Gypsy like any other doctor's office. In fact, it is nearly identical to the one they just left: same table covered with the same brown paper, same posters on the walls, same canisters on the counter beside the sink.

"Before we begin," Dr. Ryan says, "I just need to ask you a few more questions."

"Okay," Gypsy says, "but Mama's the one who knows everything."

"Some questions only you can answer."

Gypsy blushes, fusses with her bandana.

"On a scale of one to ten," Dr. Ryan begins, "how much pain would you say you're in right now?"

"I don't got no pain at all."

"Are you hungry?"

Gypsy rolls her eyes.

"Always," she says. "Problem is, I can't eat nothing but that chocolate drink with the vitamins in it. And sometimes a banana for dessert."

"Why not?"

"Real food makes me throw up. 'Cause of my condition."

"What condition is that?"

"You heard Mama. I got all kinds of conditions. It's like I collect 'em."

"Okay, but what would *you* say is wrong with you?"

Gypsy shrugs.

"I guess I'm broken. All the way broken. Like all the little parts that make me up are rotting and I can't do nothin' about it except slow it down."

"What your mother called a chromosomal defect?"

She nods.

"I see. Do you have any trouble sleeping?"

"Oh no. Mama gives me pills for that."

Dr. Ryan finds her near-toothless smile charming. There's nothing at all self-conscious about this girl; she just wants to live.

"Do you spend any time alone?" he asks.

"You mean without Mama?"

Dr. Ryan nods.

"Sometimes at night," Gypsy says. "Before bed."

"And what do you do then?"

"I like to go on the computer. Facebook,

mostly. I've got friends from all over. My goal is to have one in every state. That way, if I ever get to travel . . ."

Her voice trails off as she considers the likelihood.

"Now, Gypsy," Dr. Ryan says, "I'm going to ask you something, and I want you to be completely honest with me. Can you do that?"

"Yes sir."

"Do you ever act differently when you're alone in your room?"

"Differently how?"

"Than you would when you're with your mother. For example, do you ever get up and walk around?"

Gypsy's response comes fast: "I can't walk."

"But we just saw you walk."

"That was baby steps."

"If you can take baby steps, then you can take real steps."

Gypsy looks confused, maybe hurt.

"You think I wouldn't tell my mama if I could walk?"

"No, I'm not saying that. But maybe you wouldn't want to disappoint her?"

"Mama wants me to walk. She wants it more than anything."

Gypsy is rattled now, as if she suspects

Dr. Ryan of leading her gently toward betrayal. He decides to dial it back.

"Of course she does," he says. "So why don't you surprise her?"

"Surprise her?"

"I want you to practice walking, every night in your room. Just a little at a time until you get the hang of it. And then, when you're ready, you walk out to breakfast like it's the most natural thing in the world."

Gypsy nods, smiles: she likes having a goal.

"Perfect," Dr. Ryan says. "Now for the test."

He shuts off the overhead, takes a pen light from his jacket pocket. Gypsy follows its tiny beam around the far wall. She claps hard any time it disappears. She wants Dr. Ryan to know she is trying.

They return to the original office, find Dee Dee pacing the floor.

"Well?" she asks.

"Inconclusive," Dr. Ryan says. "If you don't have her records, I'll have to order a new battery of tests."

"Your going to make her go through all that again?" Dee Dee says. "I told you, I got it all memorized, down to the last decimal point."

"I'm sorry, but we need to have the results of her tests on record."

"You want to torture the girl over some paperwork?"

"Of course I don't want to," Dr. Ryan says. "The question is, do you?"

Dee Dee feels her face flush with heat.

"Come on, Gypsy. We're going."

They're halfway down the hall when Dr. Ryan hears Dee Dee say: "That man doesn't have the slightest idea what he's talking about."

CHAPTER 8

There is once again a small crowd gathered around Pastor Mike on the Blancharde lawn. The pastor has let his salt-and-pepper beard grow out; the worry lines on his forehead appear a little deeper, a little more jagged. Aleah and her mother stand nearby, along with Detectives Slater and Draper, and a Channel 4 news crew. Neighbors hold small, white candles in their cupped palms. There's a strong threat of rain in the air. Pastor Mike speaks without a microphone or podium.

"Like all of you, I am shocked and saddened by the sudden passing of Dee Dee Blancharde, a new and vital member of our community. Make no mistake: this is not simply a loss, it is a theft. A brutal and merciless theft. Dee Dee was stolen from us, just as all of the beautiful possibilities life represents were stolen from her. She is with God now, and I trust that everyone here is praying for her soul. To ease her passage, the First Methodist Church of Springfield will cover the full cost of her funeral."

There's a chorus of soft applause while he wipes his forehead with handkerchief. The night is unseasonably hot, and the moisture adds a tropical feel.

"As you all know, Dee Dee's daughter, Gypsy Rose Blancharde, has been missing since the night of her mother's murder. The circumstances of her disappearance remain unclear, and as the search for Gypsy is a police matter, I will turn this over to Detective Brian Slater, lead investigator on the case. But before I do, I would like to make a personal plea: Gypsy, a sweet and innocent girl, was born into this world already suffering from a greater share of ailments than most of us will experience in our lifetimes. She is sick and frail and in desperate need of her medication. I implore you to cooperate fully with the police in their investigation. If you know anything — anything at all — that might help find her, please don't hesitate to share that information with Detective Slater."

He turns from the crowd and looks directly into the nearest camera.

"And if there is somebody out there who has Gypsy, I beg you to release her to the authorities at once so that she can receive the medical attention she needs to survive. Her mortal life is at stake, but so is your soul. Saving her is the only way to save yourself."

He moves aside, gestures to Detective Slater with a slight bow of his head.

"God be with you, Pastor Mike," an onlooker calls out.

"Amen," others murmur.

Detective Slater, perspiring wildly in his checkered blazer, steps forward.

"Thank you all for coming," he begins. "I'll make my comments brief so that we can all get back to the work of finding Gypsy. Here is what we know: Gypsy was last seen at her doctor's office at four p.m. on the day she disappeared. She was last heard from in a Facebook message at nine p.m. that evening. I'm sure you're all familiar with the content of that message by now. We can't at this time say whether or not Gypsy sent the message of her own free will, or even if she sent it at all: it is of course possible that her account was hacked. What we do know with some measure of certainty is that no one has heard from her since.

"We have checked with Gypsy's medical team, and all of her prescriptions and supplies — including wheelchairs, oxygen tanks, and inhalers — are accounted for at the home. We are asking pharmacists and doctors in the area and across the country to report any attempts to buy relevant medicines without a prescription. At different times in her life, Gypsy has been diagnosed with asthma, muscular dystrophy, leukemia, and various autoimmune disorders.

"We are asking you, the public, to be vigilant. If you see something out of the ordinary, let us know. Meanwhile, we are organizing searches of local parks and open spaces. If you would like to participate, please sign up with my partner, Detective Emily Draper."

Draper, standing at the front of the crowd, waves her clipboard in the air.

"At this time," Slater continues, "we have far more questions than answers. As Pastor Mike noted, we're asking anyone with information to come forward immediately. Time is critical in any missing persons investigation, but, given Gypsy's health, it is particularly crucial in this case."

He reads out a hotline number and a URL, then hands the floor back to Pastor Mike. The rain begins to fall in fat, warm drops. Pastor Mike leads the group in prayer. Slater and Draper hang back, scanning for anyone who looks out of place, anyone who seems overly anxious, anyone who seems to be enjoying the spectacle.

When the event is over, Slater heads back to his car while Draper remains, collecting signatures. Slater is opening the driver-side door when he hears a voice calling after him. He turns to look, sees Aleah jogging up the sidewalk. The rain is pouring down now.

"Detective Slater," she says, "there's something I have to tell you."

She's drenched and doesn't seem to care. Slater feels irritated at having to stand in the rain any longer than necessary, but the girl's tone is urgent, and he can't afford to miss a potential lead.

"Why don't you tell me in the car?" he says.

Slater pops the locks, and Aleah climbs into the passenger's seat. He gives her a moment to compose herself. The windows fog over as the water on their skin and clothes turns to steam. Slater studies her out of the corner of his eye. She isn't an adult yet, but she isn't a kid, either. A difficult age. His own daughter, who disappeared from his life when her mother took her to Seattle over a decade ago, would be just a year or two younger.

"I'm getting your car all wet," Aleah says.

"That's all right," Slater tells her. "It's not really my car."

Aleah's smile is nervous, uncertain; she's clearly never talked to a cop before.

"What's your name?" Slater asks.

She dries her forehead on her sleeve, takes a deep breath.

"Aleah," she says. "Aleah Martin."

"You were friends with Gypsy?"

She nods.

"I think I was her only friend. I live across the street."

Slater remembers her now — or at least her name.

"You called 911?"

"My mother did. That Facebook message was meant for me."

Slater senses that whatever she has to say will be important, maybe game changing. He struggles to keep his voice even, calm.

"What is it you wanted to tell me?" he asks.

She hesitates, then blurts it out so fast that Slater isn't sure he's understood:

"Gypsy was seeing someone," she says.

"Gypsy?"

It seems incredible: the girl couldn't walk, and she could hardly breathe without tubes in her nose.

"Well, she had someone, sort of," Aleah says. "She called him her 'Secret Sam.' They met on a Christian dating site. I don't know which one."

"Do you know his real name?"

She shakes her head.

"I never asked. To be honest, I thought she was making him up. But now . . ."

She wipes away a tear with the heel of her palm.

"I'm sorry," she says.

Slater rests a hand on her shoulder.

"You have nothing to be sorry about," he says. "You were her friend, and you've given us our first real lead."

"But maybe if I'd said something before . . . Before Dee Dee was killed. Before Gypsy . . ."

"Listen to me," Slater says, a little more forcefully than he'd intended. "You couldn't have predicted this. No one could have. You understand?"

"I guess," she says.

Slater, not sure what more to say, takes her phone number and thanks her again. He sits for a while, watching her jog back to her house, then starts the car.

He'll have to get forensics to stop dragging their feet on Gypsy's computer.

CHAPTER 9

"All right," Slater says, "let's review."

He's standing in front of an old-fashioned chalkboard in a conference room at headquarters. Draper is there, as well as the two detectives assigned to monitor the Gypsy Rose hotline: Detective Denny Smith, who is on desk duty following an excessive force charge, and Detective Lane Schaub, who has been in plainclothes for even less time than Draper. They sit on metal folding chairs, laptops open on their knees.

"First, we've got the missing money," Slater says.

He writes *$4,000* in yellow chalk in the top left corner of the board, then turns back to the group.

"That safe still bothers me," he says. "Only someone close to her would've had access."

"Would she really have given the combination to her kid?" Smith asks.

267

"Probably not, but we found it written in a notebook at the bottom of Dee Dee's underwear drawer. Gypsy might have known where to look."

"So . . . you think the girl had an accomplice instead of a kidnapper?" Schaub asks.

"I'm just floating ideas," Slater says.

"No way she did it herself," Smith says. "Mommy had three hundred pounds on her."

"Maybe she paid someone," Schaub offers.

"Four thousand is a little short for murder," Draper says. "On top of which, Gypsy would have needed that money to live."

"If the money was even stolen," Smith says. "For all we know, Dee Dee spent it herself. Which would explain why you found the safe open: no need to lock it if there's nothing inside."

"You're right," Slater agrees. "We don't know anything for sure. All we have are hints. The money's gone, the meds are all accounted for. What scenario allows both those things to be true? No matter how many times I play it out, I keep coming back to Gypsy."

"I don't know, Brian," Draper says. "By all accounts, the girl's a little slow. It's hard to see her as a mastermind."

"That's not what I'm saying. But maybe she set something in motion without realizing it. Socially, she grew up in a very small world. She probably doesn't have a strong grasp of boundaries. Chances are she's been lonely her whole life. Maybe she was blowing off steam online and said too much to the wrong person."

"Like her Secret Sam," Schaub says.

"He's a possibility."

"If he even exists," Smith says.

"But no one we talked to described Gypsy as angry," Draper says. "If anything, they describe her as surprisingly happy."

"She and her mother were together every minute of every day. You ever spend that much time with someone and *not* want to kill them?"

"Thanks, partner," Draper chides.

"Don't worry," Smith says. "That's his divorce talking."

"Everyone swears Dee Dee and Gypsy were soul mates . . . like they lived for each other," Schaub says.

"I wonder," Slater says. "I watched that Anne-Marie footage a dozen times. There was something staged about it, like they were performing a mother-daughter skit for the thousandth time."

"The TV people probably gave them a script to work from," Draper says.

"Yeah, but it's more than that. There was something simmering. You can see little glimpses of it when they think the camera isn't on them. Gypsy looks checked out, which is understandable, but there's something forced about Dee Dee . . . like she's trying too hard to disguise her own rage."

"Kids'll do that to you," Smith says.

Draper, thinking of her partner's estranged daughter, throws Smith a biting stare.

"You want us to talk to the neighbors again?" Schaub asks.

"Can't hurt, but any relationships Dee Dee and Gypsy had here were new. We need to go further back."

"New Orleans?" Draper asks.

"That's what I'm thinking. Who knew them there? It's easy enough to keep up a façade for a few months, maybe even a few years. But time tells."

"I'll call NOPD," Draper says. "Ask them to canvas."

"Have them check on her doctors, too. Gypsy's medical records may have washed away, but the doctors didn't."

Smith lets out a sarcastic yawn: Dee Dee's murder would have been his case to solve if he hadn't put a suspected arsonist in the hospital. "This is all great, but how about some hard evidence? We get the autopsy back yet?"

"We have a preliminary report," Slater says. "Her attacker caught her by surprise. No defensive wounds. No foreign DNA under her fingernails."

"Any prints in the house?"

"One of Anne-Marie's cameramen has a DUI on his record. Otherwise, nothing."

Schaub sits up straighter, raises her hand like school is in session.

"Yes?" Slater asks.

"I know this'll sound crazy, but what if Pastor Mike has Gypsy? What if he killed Dee Dee?"

Slater and Draper smile. Smith sniggers.

"No, really," Schaub says. "Think about it. Who in Springfield is closer to them? Maybe Gypsy confided to him. Maybe he fell in love with her. Maybe he thought God could make her walk again."

"Maybe, maybe, maybe," Smith says. "The guy made her his church's charity poster child. He'd have to be some kind of stupid to turn around and butcher her mother."

"Or some kind of obsessed," Schaub counters. "It happens, you know."

Draper's computer makes a loud pinging sound. She leans closer to the screen.

"Oh my God," she says. "You aren't going to believe this."

"What is it?" Slater asks.

"A new Facebook post."

They gather around, read over her shoulder. Gypsy's avatar shows her dressed in a Cinderella outfit and flashing a fiendish grin. The post, sent from Gypsy's account, reads: "I SLASHED THAT FAT PIG AND RAPED HER SWEET INNOCENT DAUGHTER . . . HER SCREAM WAS SO LOUD LOL."

CHAPTER 10

"I want a goddamn address," Slater says. "Now!"

Detective Schaub jumps up, shuts her laptop and tucks it under one arm.

"I'll get the techies on it," she says.

"I want you on it, too. You sit there with them till we know where to send SWAT."

"Yes, sir," Schaub says, running from the room.

"It can't be Gypsy who wrote this," Draper says.

"We should answer," Smith says. "Get the bastard talking. Maybe he'll slip up."

Slater thinks it over.

"No," he decides. "Assuming it wasn't Gypsy who sent this — and that's assuming a lot for my taste — we want him to stay right where he is. Overplay our hand and he'll bolt."

"What do we do in the meantime?" Draper asks.

"Let's get Aleah Martin down here. She's Gypsy's friend. Maybe her only friend. And she has a nice face. I want her in front of a camera."

"Making a plea?" Smith asks.

Slater nods.

"What if she won't do it?" Draper asks.

"She'll do it. She's convinced herself that the whole thing is her fault. Emily, you set it up. Bring her here yourself. Door-to-door service."

"Right away," Draper says.

"And me?" Smith asks.

"You're back on the hotline."

"Waste of time. Anybody who knew anything would've called by now. All we're getting is cranks. This morning I had a guy offer to buy the meds Gypsy left behind. Then a woman tells me she saw Gypsy walking around in the background of one of those Club Med commercials. Total garbage. Unless you want to send me to Cancun, in which case . . ."

"Sorry, Denny," Slater says. "Next time, stop beating your suspect once he's unconscious."

"That was a one-time thing," Smith says. "The guy spit on my car."

"I think I hear the phone ringing," Slater says.

■ ■ ■ ■

"Sorry to pull you out of school," Draper says.

"It's all right," Aleah tells her. "Math's the worst. I wasn't even listening."

They're driving back to the station. Aleah is disheveled, her hair in a sloppy ponytail, the backpack on her lap unzipped with books and papers spilling out the top. She smells strongly of cigarettes. Draper resists the urge to lecture.

"I used to daydream in class, too," she says.

"I was thinking about Gypsy," Aleah confides. "She's pretty much all I think about now."

Draper sees this as an invitation, a chance to solicit information without conducting a formal interview. *Keep it relaxed,* she tells herself. *Just two girls chatting in a car.*

"What's Gypsy like?" she asks. "I mean, she seemed really sweet on TV, but what's she like in person?"

"She was . . . *is* real sweet," Aleah says. "She's a happy person. When we're together, it's mostly me complaining. I realize how stupid that sounds — how bad it makes me look."

"You're friends. Friends talk. They listen. There are no rules about who gets to complain more."

"I guess," Aleah says.

She turns her head, stares out the passenger-side window. Draper wonders if she's crying, or maybe trying not to. She phrases her next question carefully: "Was Gypsy different around you than she was, say, around her mother?"

"What do you mean?" Aleah asks. "Different how?"

But Draper can't say exactly what she means. She's hoping to debunk Slater's theory that Gypsy might have been involved in Dee Dee's murder. Again, she isn't sure why, but something in her needs Gypsy to be innocent.

"I don't know," Draper says. "Was she more relaxed? Did she talk about things with you that she wouldn't talk about with her mother?"

"Like boys?"

"For example . . ."

"I guess. She always got kind of quiet around Dee Dee. But everyone gets quiet around their mother."

"Especially if they're keeping secrets. Did Gypsy share any secrets with you?"

"Just the one. I told the other detective."

"Her Secret Sam?"

"Yeah. I couldn't believe it. I mean, I *didn't* believe it. I pretended to, but Gypsy knew. I keep thinking that if I'd taken her seriously . . . if I'd actually listened . . ."

Draper wants to say something to put Aleah's mind at ease, but Aleah seems to be heading somewhere important on her own — as if she's thinking out loud and has forgotten where she is or who she's talking to. Draper decides not to interrupt.

"Not just about her Secret Sam, but about everything," Aleah continues. "You said yourself: friends listen. But I didn't. Not really. Dee Dee was right."

"About what?"

Aleah squirms a little in her seat.

"I didn't really care about Gypsy," she says. "I just wanted everyone to see me as this saint looking after the local cripple. The Mother Teresa of Springfield."

"Wait, Dee Dee said that to you? In those words?"

"More or less. She said eventually I'd get bored of Gypsy and break her heart. She wanted me to stay away."

Draper remembers a sound bite from the Anne-Marie interview: *It's like she finishes my thoughts for me.* Was there a hint of sarcasm in Gypsy's voice that Draper is only picking up on now, in retrospect? As in: *She finishes my thoughts for me, but not the way I would finish them.* Maybe Slater was right: maybe the mother-daughter relationship was more troubled than Draper wanted to believe.

"For what it's worth," she says, "you sure sound to me like someone who cares. Detective Slater thinks so, too. That's why he wants you to talk to the public."

Aleah's tone turns anxious: "I always dreamed of being on TV, but not like this. What will I say?"

"Whatever's in your heart, corny as that sounds. Just pretend the camera isn't there. Pretend you're talking straight to Gypsy."

They're almost at the station now. Aleah reaches into her backpack, pulls out a hairbrush and a small makeup kit.

"Do you mind?" she asks. "I overslept this morning and had to run for the bus. I must look like I just rolled out of bed."

"Go for it," Draper says. "But I think you look very pretty."

The department's video tech sits Aleah on a stool in front of a solid blue backdrop.

"Remember, this isn't live," he says. "There's no pressure. We can reshoot as many times as you want."

But Aleah is in the zone from the moment he presses Record.

"Gypsy," she says, "if you're watching, I miss you every minute and I'd give anything to know that you're okay. And to whoever's with Gypsy, please, I'm begging you, bring her home. She needs her medicine. She needs her friends. Imagine being that sick and then the only person who's ever taken care of you is brutally murdered, and you're . . . Gypsy, you must be so afraid. You must be wondering who will look after you now. I will. I promise. Please, just come home. Whoever you are, please just bring Gypsy home so that I can take care of her."

When she's done, Draper gives her a long hug.

"That was perfect," she says.

Aleah pulls away.

"You're going to find her, right? I mean, you think there's a chance that she's . . ."

"Alive?" Draper finishes. "Yes, I do. We all do. If we didn't, we wouldn't put you on camera."

It's then that Aleah starts crying. Her sobs are deep and violent, as though she's been holding in more than she can manage for a very long time.

CHAPTER 11

Dee Dee carries two plastic cups into Gypsy's room, one full of water, the other brimming with her daughter's nightly cocktail of pills. Gypsy is already in bed, the covers pulled up to her armpits. She wears her frilly white hat with the tassels hanging down like outsize earrings.

"You're too damn old to be sleeping in that thing," Dee Dee complains.

"It keeps me warm."

"It's plenty warm in here."

"Not like that. It keeps my brain warm. It keeps me from having nightmares."

"It's your meds that do that," Dee Dee says. "Now sit up."

Gypsy obeys. Dee Dee sets the cups on the night table, stands with her arms folded. Gypsy reaches for the pills, then stops.

"Mama?" she asks.

"Yes, Gypsy?"

"How long's it gonna be this way?"

"What way is that?"

"You know what way. When am I ever gonna be better?"

Dee Dee's tone softens.

"You already are better," she says. "You just can't see it yet."

"I mean all the way better. Like other people."

Dee Dee sits on the edge of the bed, rests her hand on the blanket over Gypsy's stomach.

"Oh, sweetheart," she says. "Don't you know this is what makes you so special? You got it harder than most folks, that's true. But that's where your strength comes from. That's why you appreciate life so much more than other people."

Gypsy strikes the headboard hard with her elbows.

"But I hate my life," she says. "And I don't wanna be special. I don't want any of this shit."

Dee Dee stands back up, glares down.

"I got news for you, little girl. The world don't care what you want. No one chooses their life. You think I want any of this? You think if I'd known how things would be, I'd have brought you into this world? But you were born, and I ain't never turned my back on you. Not for a heartbeat. So how about

281

you show some goddamn gratitude? And another thing: swear like that again in front of me and I'll take a belt to your scrawny ass. I'm your mother. Don't you ever forget that. Now swallow those pills and give me a moment's peace."

Gypsy's eyes are burning, but she doesn't say anything. Instead, she places the pills one at a time under her tongue until her mouth is nearly full, then drains the cup of water. Satisfied, Dee Dee turns and walks out of the room, shutting the light on her way.

Alone, Gypsy rolls onto her side, spits the pills into the palm of her hand. She wraps them up in a Kleenex, tucks the Kleenex under her mattress.

She listens to make sure her mother isn't lurking outside, then pulls back the covers, sits up, reaches over, and switches on her computer. She slides from her bed to her wheelchair, makes her way over to the dresser, opens the bottom drawer. The glow from the monitor gives her just enough light to see by. Smiling to herself, she digs out a calico dress, a hooped skirt, and a blue satin bonnet.

Little Bo Peep: her favorite costume. It bothers her that she doesn't have the cane, but then she'll be sitting anyway — at least most of the time. She takes off her hat, ties the bonnet in place, slips the dress and skirt on over her pajamas. When she's done, she wheels herself back to the computer.

She giggles quietly as she switches over to a private window, then types in the Christian Couples URL. Nicholas's avatar shows that he isn't online. Gypsy sends him a quick message:

Need help finding my sheep!

She waits. No response. She reaches back to the bed, takes up a stuffed lamb with a black face and gray cotton fleece, and tucks it under her arm. Nicholas will like this touch, she thinks.

It's getting dark! she writes. *I'm scared!*

As she types, she realizes that her heart is beating hard and her forehead is perspiring.

I really am scared, she thinks.

Of what? Not of Nicholas. He's been so kind. He sends her emoji flowers and chocolates. He says he will take her to Australia. More than anyplace in the world, she wants to visit the Outback. She saw pictures in a *National Geographic* at the doctor's office.

No, she's afraid that he won't show up. That she will sit there alone staring at the camera light on her computer until the sun comes up. She's afraid of having no one to talk to but her mother and doctor and all the people who want to fix her. She's afraid that Nicholas will want to fix her, too.

She types:

Helloooo?? Are you there???

But before she can hit Send, a green dot appears under Nicholas's picture, and then the picture is gone, and it's Nicholas himself smiling at her. He's wearing an eye patch and a pirate's hat, and there's a plastic cockatoo perched on his shoulder.

CHAPTER 12

On a Tuesday afternoon, they have the park to themselves. Aleah wheels Gypsy along the asphalt path that circles the lake. Gypsy is wearing a sunhat and long sleeves despite the eighty-degree temperature. She points to a row of ducks on the water.

"I wish I could swim with them," she says.

"Maybe I could take you out sometime. They rent paddle boats here on the weekends."

"I was hoping someone else would take me," Gypsy says. She laughs, covering her mouth with both hands, a habit meant to hide her crumbling teeth.

"Who'd you have in mind?" Aleah asks, playing along. She imagines Gypsy will name some popular heartthrob — Justin Timberlake, or maybe Ryan Gosling.

"Can you keep a secret?" Gypsy asks.

"You know I can."

"I've got a Secret Sam."

"A what?"

"A boyfriend, silly. No one is supposed to know. That's why he's a *secret.*"

Aleah wants to be patient, but she is not in the mood for another of Gypsy's daydreams. Her own boyfriend broke up with her less than a week ago, and she just learned that her SAT scores won't help her chances of going to college — especially out of state. No way can she stay stuck in Springfield another year!

"A boyfriend?" she asks. "How? I mean, no offense, but you never leave the house unless you're with me or your mother."

"He visits me at home."

Aleah rolls her eyes.

"Is this some kind of riddle, Gypsy? 'Cause I didn't get a whole lot of sleep last night, so you might have to help me out."

Gypsy giggles, her hands once again flying up to cover her mouth.

"A riddle," she says. "I like that. Let's make it a riddle. I'll give you a hint: sometimes you visit me the same way."

Just tell me already, Aleah thinks. She's about to change the subject completely when it dawns on her: Gypsy must have a crush on one of her Facebook friends. Something about this makes Aleah sad; her own problems seem suddenly trivial.

"You're chatting with someone online?" she says.

"He wouldn't be a Secret Sam if all we did was chat."

Now Aleah is concerned. She doesn't know how, exactly, but she's sure that poor Gypsy is about to get her heart broken.

"What do you mean? What more can you do on Facebook?"

"Who said anything about Facebook?"

Aleah wheels Gypsy over to a bench and parks the chair so that they can sit facing one another.

"What's going on, Gypsy?"

"Gosh," Gypsy says, batting her eyes. "Why the long face? Is someone jealous?"

Gypsy is in playful mode, which means it will be hard to get any real information out of her. Aleah gathers herself, tries to be the friend she imagines Gypsy wants.

"I'm not jealous," she says. "I'm happy for you. But the suspense is killing me."

Gypsy looks over each shoulder, adjusts the tubes in her nose.

"Not fair," she complains. "I can't see the water from here."

Aleah stands, wheels Gypsy to the end of the bench and positions her chair so that they can sit side by side, both facing the lake.

"Now tell me!" she says.

"You're sure you can keep a secret?" Gypsy teases.

"Of course."

"You're the only person I'm telling, so if you-know-who finds out . . ."

"I won't say a thing."

"All right. I signed up on a dating site."

Aleah feels her stomach sink a little. Gypsy notices.

"It's not like that," she says. "It's a *Christian* dating site."

Aleah does her best to appear comforted.

"Aren't you a little young for a dating site?" she asks.

"It's not like they check your ID. And it's just flirting, mostly. Or it was."

"What is it now?"

"I told you . . . I've got someone. And I need your help."

"Help with what?"

Gypsy flashes a coy grin.

"You got your driver's license, right?"

Aleah sees where this is going.

"Gypsy, I can't —"

"You wouldn't have to take me far. Just to the ice cream parlor on Pearl Street. He wants to meet me for real."

"Why doesn't he just pick you up?"

"You know why. Mama can't find out.

288

Besides which, I got butterflies. I need you with me."

Better and better, Aleah thinks. She sees herself playing chaperone, sitting beside Gypsy in a cramped booth, looking across at . . . She hates herself for being mean, but what kind of guy would date Gypsy?

If there even is a guy, she thinks. Maybe Gypsy is playing some kind of game. Maybe she doesn't know herself that she's playing. Maybe this is a fantasy spun out of control. Whatever the case, Aleah does not want to encourage her. Then again, she doesn't want to discourage her, either. It's hard enough being Gypsy Rose Blancharde.

"I want to help," Aleah says, "but —"

"No!" Gypsy cuts her off. "No buts! Please, I'm begging you. I have to see him now, before I can't anymore."

"What does that mean?"

"I told you, I have to have another surgery on my eyes. What if something goes bad?"

"Nothing will —"

"The doctor's hand could slip. Or I could have some kind of allergic reaction. Or maybe he just won't be able to fix me. I have to see him while I still can. That way, if we end up together, I'll be able to picture him when I hear his voice. I'll be able to see his smile. I'll know what he looks like when he

289

looks at me."

Aleah hesitates. Her instincts are screaming at her to stay away, but Gypsy looks so desperate, and in the end she has a point: how many opportunities will a girl in Gypsy's situation have? *If* this is even a real opportunity.

"All right," she says. "But maybe you better tell me a little about him first."

"Thank you, thank you, thank you," Gypsy says.

And then she goes quiet for a long beat. When Aleah looks over, she sees that her friend is crying.

CHAPTER 13

"Ow!" Gypsy says, jerking her head away.

"See, that's how you get cut," Dee Dee says. "Then you blame me. Now hold still."

They're in the living room, Gypsy seated on a plastic stool with a short back, Dee Dee standing behind her, working the hair clippers. The TV is on in the background, tuned to a hospital-themed soap opera Dee Dee calls her "story."

"Why can't we just let it grow?" Gypsy asks. "I think I'd look pretty with long hair."

"You look pretty now."

"But if I had hair, I wouldn't have to wear that hat you hate so much."

"We've been over this, Gypsy. It's the cancer won't let you grow your hair. I'm guessing you don't wanna shed like a dog?"

"Maybe I wouldn't. We could try it. Just the one time."

"Enough already, Gypsy. Under my roof, we keep things neat and tidy."

Gypsy thinks: *Don't you mean the church's roof?* Which reminds her . . .

"About what Pastor Mike said, I was thinking —"

"Don't start with that now. He shouldn't have said nothing without asking me first. Now quit squirming. I'm about done here."

She runs a finger over her daughter's nearly bare scalp.

"I don't like this mole you've got here one bit," she says. "Keeps growing on me."

"But Mama," Gypsy says, "who turns down a free trip to Disney World?"

"Maybe you should've thought things through before you pulled that stunt the last time. Damn near gave me a heart attack."

"But I learned my lesson, Mama. Nothing like that'll happen again."

"You bet it won't. I should've had that man arrested. Who runs off with a child?"

"He didn't know how young I was on account of the costume. And we didn't run off, we —"

"Drop it now, Gypsy," Dee Dee says. "You're working my last nerve, and it ain't even noon yet."

But Gypsy's mind is already drifting back to last summer, to the time when the man in the orange jumpsuit with the fake bionic leg almost set her free.

The trip had been a gift from their New Orleans church. Pastor Dan had noticed Dee Dee and Gypsy's shared love of sci-fi movies, from *The Thing* (the classic 1951 version) to *Close Encounters* to *E.T.* (though that one always made Gypsy cry). The pastor started a fundraiser to send them to Intergalactic Con in Naples, Florida. He chose the conference because it featured a space-themed art show — a contest that all attendees with an artistic bent were encouraged to enter. As he was seeing them off at the airport, Pastor Dan put a hand on Gypsy's shoulder and said: "Bring the prize home, kiddo."

She'd had a month to prepare, during which time she was never without a pencil in her hand. The idea came to her early on: a large-scale design of the first human colony on Mars. Instead of houses or apartments, she imagined a futuristic hybrid: ranch-style homes with earth-colored metallic exteriors stacked in structures that looked like ultra-sleek parking garages. High-speed conveyor belts replaced sidewalks, and there were no streets at all since cars would be able to fly. There were no zoos, either, since animals of every stripe would be domesticated, and she did away with hospitals and cemeteries because disease and death would be things of the past.

Advertising, however, would be alive and well in the future. She imagined billboards hovering in midair; spotlights projecting logos for everything from brand-name beverages to three-dimensional video games; jingles playing continuously on a public radio that could never be shut off (though Gypsy wasn't sure how to convey the latter without using words).

The final drawing filled a poster-sized canvas and looked like an elaborate blueprint with minuscule detail lurking in every crevice.

"I gotta give it to you," Dee Dee said, "you sure worked on this one. Can't imagine what you're gonna do with yourself now."

"Maybe I'll be an architect," Gypsy said.

"Maybe you will at that."

It was the only time Gypsy could remember her mother sounding proud.

The first two days of the conference were the very best of Gypsy's life. Their room was on the top floor of an eighteen-story hotel, and all Gypsy could see from the window was pure-blue sky and endless water. The jam-packed lineup of events included an alien-themed comedy show, a staged light saber fight between two stuntmen who worked on *The Phantom Menace,* an exhibit of alternate designs for the *Millennium Falcon,* and a screening of deleted scenes from all three *Back to the Future* movies.

"I don't want this to ever end," Gypsy told her mother.

But it wasn't just the spectacle and setting: for the first time in her life, Gypsy did not feel out of place. True, she was one of very few participants in a wheelchair, and maybe the only one with an oxygen tank, but nobody seemed to notice. It was OK to be strange with so many robots and storm troopers and space creatures roaming the hotel. Here, people talked to her without the slightest trace of pity or revulsion.

That was how Gypsy met Robert: he just walked up to her and started talking.

It was during the costume ball on the last night of the conference. Gypsy was dressed as an alien, and Dee Dee as the Sigourney Weaver character from the movies. The winners of the art contest had just been announced. Gypsy's drawing placed third out of eighty-seven entries. It wasn't enough to win her the $1,000 prize, but it did earn her a ribbon, and they even put a photo of

Gypsy and the drawing up on a projector screen. Gypsy was ecstatic . . . until she looked up and saw her mother's face.

"There weren't two drawings better than yours," Dee Dee said. "Not even close. Those judges robbed us, and I ain't gonna go quietly."

She walked off, leaving Gypsy alone on the edge of the crowded dance floor. Gypsy sat and sipped from her Shirley Temple, feeling like she might cry for the first time all weekend.

"Excuse me," a voice said.

She looked up, saw the man in the orange jumpsuit with the fake robot-leg standing over her.

"I couldn't help but overhear," he said. "I agree with that woman: you were robbed."

Gypsy wondered if the man could see her blushing in the room's dim light. For her part, she could just make out his features. He had a nice face — the kind of thin, angular face she liked to draw.

"That's nice of you," she said. "But third place ain't bad. Not with all those people who entered."

The man smiled.

"My name's Robert," he said. "It's nice to meet such a gifted artist, Gypsy Rose."

And then, without knowing she would,

Gypsy repeated a line she'd heard in countless movies: "Why don't we get out of here, Robert?"

Robert?"

CHAPTER 14

It wasn't the kind of thing she'd have said,
or even thought to say, in any other setting.

Robert didn't hesitate:

"Do you have someplace in mind?" he
asked.

Gypsy scanned the ballroom. Her mother
was nowhere in sight.

"Someplace away from all these people,"
Gypsy said.

"My thinking exactly."

He wheeled her out of the ballroom and
down a long corridor to the bank of eleva-
tors. Gypsy resisted the urge to look over
her shoulder. She wished Robert would
push faster. It wasn't until the elevator door
closed behind them that she knew she'd
made her escape, though she couldn't say
exactly what she'd escaped from, or what
she was running to. After a quick wave of
relief, she was suddenly very afraid. She
glanced up at Robert. The harsh overhead

light aged him ten years (he was as old as Dee Dee — maybe older), and his face wasn't so much thin and angular as gaunt and pale.

"Are you cold?" he asked.

She hadn't noticed that her limbs were shaking. Now that he'd pointed it out, she couldn't think of anything else. The trembling spread through her body and into her jaw so that her teeth were knocking together loud enough for him to hear.

"I'll be OK," she managed.

He put his hands on her shoulders, rubbed her back with his thumbs until the doors opened.

No going back now, Gypsy thought.

His room was only on the sixth floor and didn't face the water. It smelled a little musty, and though the bed was made, there were clothes strewn all over the floor and dresser and desk.

"Sorry," he said. "I wasn't expecting company."

And then Gypsy noticed something that put her at ease, or at least more at ease than she had been. The surface of his nightstand was covered in pill bottles, with the bottles stacked in columns reaching three or four high. *Maybe,* Gypsy thought, *he's sick. Like me, but not as bad. He's sick like me but has no one to help him.*

Thinking this made her want to be his princess, even if he was more frog than prince.

"Would you like something to drink?" he asked. "I have a nice bottle of Irish whiskey that should warm you right up."

"Um, OK," Gypsy said. She wasn't about to tell him that she'd never had so much as a drop of alcohol, any more than she'd confess to this being her first time alone with a man.

He went into the bathroom and came back carrying two plastic cups, the kind hotels give you to gargle with, already filled to the brim with brown liquid. He handed one over.

"Obliged," Gypsy said: another expression she'd picked up from the movies.

"Cheers," he said, raising his cup.

"Cheers," Gypsy echoed.

In her short life, Gypsy had tasted syrups and serums of every kind, but nothing that burned quite like this. She could feel her eyes watering, her cheeks turning red.

Robert smiled, sat across from her on the edge of the bed.

"Take your time with it," he said. "Whiskey's an acquired taste."

"What's that mean?"

"It grows on you," Robert said.

He leaned forward, elbows on his knees, so that their faces were just inches apart. She could smell the alcohol on him, imagined that he could smell it on her, too.

"Tell me about yourself, Gypsy Rose," he said.

Gypsy grinned, looked around the room as though there might be some other Gypsy Rose lurking in a corner.

"What should I tell?" she asked.

"Well, for starters, where are you from?"

Gypsy took a slow sip of whiskey. This time there was no burn — just a pleasant warmth sliding down into her body.

"New Orleans, to start with," she said.

"Ah," Robert said. "The Big Easy."

"Wasn't nothing easy about it," Gypsy corrected. "Katrina ripped my home up and blew it away, just like in *The Wizard of Oz.* I live in Missouri now. Sounds like misery, but it's a nice enough place. The people are nice, anyway. It was my old pastor set up this trip. He encourages me with my art."

She noticed herself saying *me* and *my,* quietly avoiding any hint of her mother, who, she realized, must have started searching by now.

"There are some good things about it, too," she continued. "Missouri, I mean.

301

Like, I ain't seen a single cockroach since I been there. In New Orleans, they're big as your fist, and most of 'em fly. There's no getting used to that no matter how long you live. And it's quiet in Missouri, especially at night. In New Orleans, I slept with a fan on just to block out the street noise, but in Missouri there's no noise to block out. Sometimes it's almost too quiet, like in a horror movie right before the girl gets attacked."

She knew that she was talking too much, that she should stop and ask about his life, but she'd slipped into a rhythm she couldn't break. Maybe it was the whiskey, which had her feeling a little like the meds her mother gave her at night, except that she wasn't tired. This was more like the wide-awake time just before she got tired, when thoughts were like feathers in her head and she was chasing them all around.

Robert let her go on a while longer before he interrupted.

"That's a dandy of a wheelchair," he said.

She gave him a vacant look: no one had ever complimented one of her chairs before.

"Sleek and chic," he continued. "Like something from the future. Like the type of conveyance people might use in your Mars colony."

"I hadn't thought much about that,"

Gypsy said. "I guess you're right."

"Tell me," he said, "can you walk?"

"You mean without the chair?"

He nodded. Something about him had changed. His eyes were stretched wide, and he looked like he'd never wanted anything so bad as for her to give the right answer.

"Why would I wheel myself around if I could just get up and walk?" she asked.

He didn't seem to hear. He bent forward, set his cup on the floor, undid the Velcro straps that held his fake bionic leg in place.

"You see," he said, "I can take this off whenever I want, and then I'm just like everybody else. But you . . . you're special. You can't be anything but special."

"Special?"

"Unique. No matter what, your experience of this world will never be like everybody else's."

He took her half-full cup and set it on the floor beside his own. Then he touched her hand. He was so sincere. So eager. Gypsy felt the fear creeping back. She tried to concentrate, but his face kept dropping out of focus.

"I'm going to kiss you now," he said. "And then I'm going to lift you onto that bed."

Gypsy gripped the arms of her chair, let his lips touch hers. His stubble scratched her skin; what he was doing with his tongue confused her. She thought it could only be the whiskey that kept her from shaking all over again.

"May I?" he asked, forcing one arm awkwardly under her legs.

And then, before she could answer, she heard her mother's voice tearing through the hall outside, followed by a furious banging on Robert's door.

"Gypsy Rose, goddamn it, I know you're in there!"

Gypsy looked up at Robert. His face was turning colors and there was a saliva bubble swelling out the side of his mouth. She wondered if it was possible to be rescued and taken prisoner at the same time.

CHAPTER 15

Aleah sits with her mother in the front pew of Springfield Methodist. The church is full, but the crowd is so quiet that Aleah feels alone with Pastor Mike and his words. He stands behind a large mahogany coffin, his open palms raised skyward.

"Dee Dee Blancharde," he intones, "was taken from this world far too soon. She was taken from this community before any of us really got a chance to know her, though certainly we know about her. We know about her devotion to her daughter. We saw enough of Dee Dee to know that her actions were in keeping with her values. Despite the demands placed on her as full-time caretaker, a duty she fulfilled out of love rather than obligation, she served this church with the fervor and dedication of someone who'd grown up among us."

Aleah has trouble concentrating. She's never been this close to a coffin before. She can't stop picturing the body inside, the bones and flesh lying still with no hope of ever moving again. In life, Dee Dee had been all motion, always fidgeting, always jumping up to fetch something for someone: a glass of lemonade or a plate of cookies for guests; a pillow for Gypsy when her back started to ache from so much sitting.

"Dee Dee lived not for herself," Pastor Mike continues, "but for others. She lived first and foremost for her daughter, Gypsy Rose. If you asked Dee Dee how she herself felt on a particular day, she might tell you that Gypsy had or hadn't slept well, that a symptom of her daughter's illness had or hadn't improved. Never a word about her own plight, her own suffering."

Aleah thinks: *Of course she never complained. Not to you. You were Dee Dee Blancharde's cash cow.* The thought surprises her. She feels confused, ashamed, and not very Christian. The plain truth is that she never much liked Dee Dee. The outsize woman, now resting just a few feet away in her outsize coffin, made Aleah uncomfortable. She had been overbearing, smothering. A control freak who always found a way to make herself the center of attention. Pastor Mike was right in saying that she didn't talk about herself, but it was always

Dee Dee's energy, Dee Dee's anxiety that dominated a room. The fact that she died doesn't change who she was in life. Somehow, Aleah had thought it would. She'd thought it would be easier to love the dead, whose sins and shortcomings were once and for all behind them.

"The greatest way to honor Dee Dee," Pastor Mike goes on, "is to care for her daughter as she no longer can. Dee Dee was a savior to that girl, and a friend to this church."

Aleah realizes that she does not much like Pastor Mike, either. He speaks in preacher-voice even when he isn't preaching, and there is something self-congratulatory about his goodness, like he's always hovering above himself, smiling and approving. These thoughts frighten Aleah: here she is in a church, thinking ill of a dead woman and a pastor. She may have her doubts about the character of certain people, but she has no doubt that hell is real.

"I know many of you have participated in search parties, donning your galoshes and rolling up your sleeves to comb through damp fields and marshes on scalding summer days. To tell you the truth, I'm glad that you've found nothing. I'm more than glad. I'm encouraged. I feel it in my bones:

Gypsy Rose is alive."

Aleah's mother gives her hand a little squeeze. Aleah does her best to smile.

"We must prepare, then, to welcome Gypsy Rose Blancharde back into our community and into our hearts. Gypsy, a simple and innocent soul who never harmed and would never dream of harming any living creature. Gypsy, a fragile young girl with an infectious laugh and a warm smile for anyone she meets. Gypsy, with a passion for cinema and a gift for art. Gypsy . . ."

Aleah can't take anymore. She thinks: *Don't pretend you know her. Gypsy isn't simple. She isn't innocent — not the way you mean. She's a person. A real, living human being.*

Almost as though it's happening without her, Aleah leaps up and runs out of the church, letting the double doors slam shut in her wake. Her mother finds her a few moments later, sitting on a bench in the small square opposite Springfield Methodist, weeping and beating on her legs with both fists.

"Aleah," her mother says, "stop that. Stop it right now."

She kneels down, grabs her daughter's wrists.

"I wish it was me," Aleah yells.

"You wish what was you?"

"I wish it was me instead of Gypsy, wherever she is. Whatever he's doing to her. I didn't believe her. I wish it was me. It should be me."

"Aleah, honey, what are you talking about?"

"I'm no good. Dad's right. Dee Dee was right. There's nothing good about me. I have no reason to —"

"Your father never said —"

"You think I don't hear you every night? He said it and he meant it and he's right."

"Aleah, I need you to calm down and tell me what's going on."

"She's alive," Aleah says. "She's alive, and what he's doing to her is worse than what he did to Dee Dee. It should be me. I'll never forgive myself. I don't care how long . . ."

She's out of breath now, gasping and sobbing at once. Her mother climbs up onto the bench, takes Aleah in her arms, and kisses her forehead.

"Let's go home," she says.

CHAPTER 16

It's eight in the morning, and Slater sits in the break room picking through the remains of last night's takeout: a watery pad Thai that he dresses up now with ketchup and red pepper. While he eats, he again reads through the meager case file labeled *Gypsy Rose Blancharde*. He wonders if the search might lead them to New Orleans, if someone from Gypsy's past came to retrieve her. Lately, his mind has been spinning out theories faster than he can reject them. *Theories are easy to come by,* he thinks. *Facts, not so much.*

He feels as though it's been weeks since he slept. Last night, at three a.m., he gave up trying, slipped out of bed, and drove around the streets of Springfield, hoping that Gypsy's captor, if she had in fact been captured, might take her out for some air in the dead of night. He squinted at every porch, got out and peered over fences. He kept at it all the way until his shift started.

Alone in the break room, he feels his eyes shutting. He pushes aside his plate, folds his arms on the table, and starts to rest his head when Draper comes bolting through the doorway.

"Nicholas Godejohn," she says.

She's panting like she's run up multiple flights of stairs though her desk sits just a short distance down the hall.

"Who?" Slater asks, rubbing his eyes.

"Nicholas Godejohn, 512 Crestview Road."

"Emily, take a breath. Start from the top."

"Forensics tracked him down through the credit card he used to pay for Christian Couples."

"You're saying . . ."

"I'm saying it's him. Gypsy's Secret Sam."

Slater stands as though in a daze, then grabs up his coffee mug and swallows the dregs so quickly that brown liquid dribbles down his chin.

"Get the team together," he says. "I'll call SWAT."

Nicholas Godejohn wakes, lifts off his night mask, sees that Gypsy is already up. He runs a hand over her side of the bed, finds it still warm. The clock says nine fifteen. *Probably making my breakfast,* he tells himself. *The way I showed her.*

He smiles to himself, shuts his eyes, and drops his head back onto the pillow. True, their relationship got off to a rocky start — killing a nearly four-hundred-pound woman had been messier and more physically taxing than he'd imagined, and Gypsy had not been as grateful as he would have liked — but there is no denying that, overall, Nicholas has done well. *Pick 'em fresh from the tree,* his second foster father used to say. And they don't come any fresher than Gypsy Rose Blancharde. In a way, it's like her life started when she met him. Before that, she'd been living someone else's life, a life someone else had made up for her. She was his now to train, to raise up right.

Of course, there are rough patches ahead of them, too. They will have to get clear of Missouri, then get out of the country altogether. Nicholas has a place picked out in Canada, a trailer on a large plot of land in the northern Rockies. He can rent it for a song from his co-worker's father who is too ill now for hunting and fishing, let alone skiing. Nicholas is just waiting for his last check from the bottling plant to clear. His savings, coupled with the four thousand dollars from Dee Dee's safe, should last them

312

a good while.

It's the travel that scares him. Stopping for gas and eating at diners and checking into motels — all those places where Gypsy might be recognized. Lucky for him, the girl loves to wear disguises.

He feels air moving in his stomach, listens for signs of Gypsy bringing his breakfast. He is keeping her culinary lessons simple for now: instant oatmeal with frozen straw-berries mixed in; instant coffee with just a dollop of creamer. He'd had to teach her how to boil water. When they get to Canada, he'll teach her more: how to gut and fry the fish he catches; how to make a proper duck stew; how to pick chokecherries and turn them into jam. Things he learned from a string of foster families all across the state of Wyoming. They will live off the land as much as possible, grow old in the company of Mother Nature.

He hears a crashing from somewhere inside the house, a metal pot hitting the floor and clattering around. He can't blame her: in a way, she's still learning how to walk. He considers going out to help her but doesn't yet have the energy to rouse himself.

Then he hears something else, this time coming from outside the house, from just outside his bedroom window, in the narrow space between his bungalow and his neighbor's fence. A crackling sound, like static on a radio, followed quickly by a string of hushed curses. He sits up, slaps himself awake, goes to the window, and pulls the shade back an inch. There's a man dressed all in black standing maybe a yard away, fiddling with some kind of handheld device. Still drowsy, Nicholas thinks it must be the gas man, but then he realizes: employees of the gas company don't carry side arms.

He steps back, tugs the shade as far open as he dares, cranes his neck. There are cop cars with their lights flashing and sirens muted clogging his quiet residential street. He pulls his hand away, lets the shade fall shut, and hops around in his bare feet as though the floor were made of burning coals.

"Oh shit, oh shit, oh shit," he says.

He looks furiously around the room, spots his jeans lying crumpled in a corner, pulls them on. He has no time to worry about a shirt or shoes. He jets down the hallway and out the back door, finds his yard crowded with men in black masks brandishing machine guns. He throws his hands in the air, but they tackle him anyway, pushing him face-forward into the dirt.

Once the cuffs are on, they roll him onto his back. He looks up, sees a man in plain clothes staring down at him.

"Where is she?" Slater asks.

There's no point in playing dumb.

"Inside," Nicholas says. "But she ain't who you think she is."

CHAPTER 17

It's been a week since Dr. Ryan saw Gypsy and her mother. He spends his lunch hour searching for Gypsy's New Orleans physician, calling colleagues in the parish where they lived before coming to Springfield. He is about to give up when a hospital administrator reads him the number for Gypsy's primary care physician, a Dr. John Wyatt.

He has just fifteen minutes before his next patient is scheduled. He dials Dr. Wyatt's office, and a woman's voice asks if he wouldn't mind holding. Before he can answer, he's listening to a Muzak version of Billy Joel's "Piano Man." He reviews the results of Gypsy's blood work while he waits. The tests show tell-tale signs of malnutrition. Her electrolyte levels are perilously low, and she's deficient in almost every essential vitamin. Her complete blood count, however, gives no indication of leukemia. Dr. Ryan is stumped.

"Dr. Hall's office," a new, more gravelly female voice says. "I apologize for the wait. How may I help you today?"

"Dr. Hall? I'm sorry, I was trying to reach Dr. Wyatt."

"Good luck with that," the woman says. "He retired a few months back. Last I heard he was hiking the Appalachian Trail. He's seventy years old but still fit as a fiddle, that one."

"I see. My name is Dr. Daniel Ryan. I'm calling from Springfield, Missouri. It seems I've inherited one of his patients. Would you by any chance have access to his records?"

"In my head I might. Katrina wiped out our paper trail, but I've been a nurse in this office going on fifteen years. Who's your patient?"

So Dee Dee had been telling at least a partial truth: Katrina really did erase Gypsy's medical history.

"Her name is Gypsy Rose Blancharde," Dr. Ryan says.

"Oh, I remember Gypsy all right," the nurse says. "How could I forget? She was here so much we thought about charging her momma rent."

Dr. Ryan perks up: this is the first glimmer of hope in an otherwise wasted hour.

"Do you remember what Dr. Wyatt was

treating Gypsy for?"

"Gosh, I'd have to say just about everything at one time or another. I remember a visit where she had high blood pressure, then another where she barely had a pulse."

"But no specific diagnosis?"

"I know she had asthma. And eczema, maybe. That girl's skin would flake like the devil."

"Nothing more serious? No cancer? No autoimmune illness? No chromosomal abnormalities?"

"No sir, nothing like that. Gypsy was all symptoms and no disease."

Dr. Ryan does his best not to sound accusatory.

"Do you know then how she wound up in a wheelchair and an oxygen mask?"

"Well, you'd have to ask Dr. Wyatt about that. Like I said, Gypsy had no shortage of things wrong with her. They just didn't add up to any one illness."

Dr. Ryan decides to press a little further.

"If you don't mind my asking, what kind of physician was Dr. Wyatt?"

"Oh, he was a plain old family practitioner."

"I guess I'm asking more about —"

"I know what you're asking about. Dr. Wyatt wasn't a quack, I can tell you that much. Knew his medicine inside and out. But he was . . . fearful."

"Fearful?"

"Mostly, Dr. Wyatt did what he could not to get sued. Especially once the end was in sight. He wanted to get out the door without any headaches chasing after him. And no one put him on edge like that girl's mother. She had civil court written all over her. I'm telling you this for your sake. And Gypsy's, too."

"I see," Dr. Ryan says. "Thank you very much. You've been a big help."

He hangs up with just a few minutes left until his next appointment. His first thought is that he would like to find this Dr. Wyatt and wring his neck. He's certain now: Gypsy isn't sick so much as she's being made sick by her mother. But why? Why would any parent deliberately manufacture a sick child?

Dee Dee, he reasons, is like a stage mother gone to the opposite extreme. Instead of pressuring her daughter to be perfect, Dee Dee burdens Gypsy with debilitating illness. Instead of organizing her life around Gypsy's auditions and classes and recitals, she organizes her life around Gypsy's doctor visits. Like a stage mother, Dee Dee controls her daughter's every action, but unlike a stage mother, Dee Dee has an airtight defense should Gypsy ever choose to rebel. To all appearances, Dee Dee isn't forcing Gypsy to do anything against her will: rather, she is selflessly shepherding her daughter through the most difficult life imaginable.

Dee Dee must have worked hard to create a universe where no one would suspect that there was nothing at all wrong with Gypsy. To begin with, she would have needed to limit the witnesses — get rid of the father, if he was ever in the picture; alienate any extended family; insist on homeschooling. Later, when Gypsy was old enough to understand, she must have convinced the child herself that she was sick. She must have fabricated evidence. Poisoned Gypsy's food so that eating came to mean nausea, vomiting; smothered her in her sleep and called it apnea; injected her with urine to stimulate infections; induced seizures with drugs or sleep deprivation.

Finally, Dee Dee would have had to convince the medical community. She likely shopped around until she found the right doctor, one who saw her as a concerned and loving parent who would gladly trade her own life for her child's health if only such a thing were possible. A doctor who promised to rise to the challenge, find the rare diagnosis that fit Gypsy's extraordinary range of symptoms.

By making Gypsy sick, Dee Dee had created a need that only she could fill. She'd given her life a vital purpose, a purpose that wouldn't end once her child was grown, though it might very well end with her child's death. At which point, Dee Dee would become a martyr.

Not that Dee Dee consciously thinks in these terms. Dee Dee, Dr. Ryan understands, is the one who's ill. She suffers from a psychological disease that allows her to believe in her daughter's sickness. It's as though there are two separate Dee Dees: the one who poisons and starves her daughter, and the one who fights to keep her daughter alive. The savior might be vaguely aware of the villain's existence, but the two have never met face-to-face.

But Gypsy is still young. There is time to stop this before the damage proves irreversible.

Dr. Ryan turns to the front page of Gypsy's file, picks up the phone, and dials Dee Dee's number. An automated message informs him that she is unavailable. He waits for the tone.

"Hello, Ms. Blancharde," he says. "This is

Dr. Ryan calling. I have Gypsy's test results, and I need to speak with you in person as soon as possible. Please call my office to schedule an appointment. And please do not plan to bring Gypsy; I'd like to speak with you one on one. Again, this is urgent."

He hangs up with the sinking feeling that Dee Dee will never return his call.

CHAPTER 18

It's Dee Dee who answers the door. Aleah
had hoped to find Gypsy waiting on the
front walk, ready to go.

"Come in, come in," Dee Dee says. "Her
highness is still getting ready."

"Thank you," Aleah says, stepping inside.

The air conditioner is pumping full blast,
and the abrupt change in temperature gives
Aleah goose bumps up and down her arms.
The Blancharde home is looking more and
more lived in. There are supermarket flyers
piled high on the table, clothes and linens
draped all over Aleah's spare wheelchairs,
dirty dishes stacked on the floor in front of
the couch.

"Gypsy," Dee Dee calls. "Your ride is
here."

The dig isn't lost on Aleah: she isn't
Gypsy's friend, she's a means of transportation.

"Be right there," Gypsy yells back.

Dee Dee turns to Aleah.

"So what movie are you two seeing again?" she asks.

The question sounds like pure suspicion.

"It's a French sci-fi flick," Aleah says. "Gypsy picked it."

"Of course she did. That girl and her fantasies. Not that I'm much better. That's one thing she gets from me. I'm sure there are other things, but this is one of those days when I just can't see them. Girl's been working my last nerve since breakfast."

Aleah nods. Dee Dee, she notices, isn't in much better shape than her home. Her hair looks slept on, there are bits of crusted food clinging to her gray shift, and her bare feet are marked with bony, reddish lumps.

"Remind me what theater it is you're going to?" Dee Dee asks.

Somehow, Aleah is certain that Dee Dee doesn't really need reminding.

"The Canterbury," Aleah says. "Over on Pearl."

This is the story she and Gypsy have rehearsed.

"Right, the Canterbury. I've driven by it. Looks fancy as hell from the outside, what with all those columns and that ivy. Even if the ivy is fake."

"It's just a normal theater on the inside,"

324

Aleah says.

"Well, maybe someday I'll see for myself," Dee Dee says.

Is she asking to be invited? Aleah wonders.

There's a brief lull before Dee Dee asks her next question: "You've had your license for how long now?"

"Going on six months," Aleah says.

"I told you, Mama, she's a real good driver."

It's Gypsy, wheeling herself into the living room, flashing Aleah a big, nervous smile.

"My gosh, look at you," Dee Dee says.

Gypsy is decked out in a pale blue ruched dress with a cloud print — the one she wears to church on holidays and special occasions. She's accessorized with an imitation pearl necklace, a black handbag, and gold-colored shoes. For a bit of flair, she's put on two different shades of lipstick: dark violet on her upper lip, scarlet on the lower.

"You know it's gonna be dark in that theater, right?" Dee Dee says. "Ain't no one gonna see you."

"Out of the house is out of the house, Mama," Gypsy reasons.

"Well, I wish you'd told me you were gonna doll yourself up. I could've helped some. You look like a French Quarter whore."

Aleah blushes. Gypsy pretends not to hear.

"And what are you wearing them heels for?" Dee Dee continues. "You know you can't walk as it is."

"We better be going," Aleah says. "I hate missing the previews."

She wheels Gypsy out to the car, helps her into the passenger's seat, and folds the wheelchair into the trunk. As they're pulling away from the curb, Aleah says: "Your mother's wrong. I think you look very pretty."

"I just hope *he* thinks so," Gypsy says. "I never been so jittery in all my life."

"Aren't you going to at least tell me his real name?" Aleah asks.

"I promised I wouldn't."

"So I'm just supposed to call him Secret Sam? Like Secret is his first name? *Hey Secret, how's it going? That's a nice jacket you're wearing, Secret.*"

Gypsy giggles.

"If he wants to tell you, that's different," she says. "But a promise is a promise."

Aleah thinks:

Dee Dee was right about one thing . . . I'm just the transportation.

They sit in a booth by the window, Gypsy facing the door. There's an empty ice cream sundae bowl and two empty cups of hot chocolate on the table in front of them. Gypsy, unused to the sugar and syrup and cream, is feeling a little queasy. They've been here over an hour, but it feels like longer since either of them spoke. Gypsy breaks the silence.

"He'll be here," she says. "I must've got the time wrong."

"You want to text him?" Aleah asks.

"I told you, he ain't got a phone."

Gypsy taps her fingers tunelessly on the table. Aleah wants to comfort her — or rather, she wants to want to comfort her. Really, Aleah is having doubts about the existence of this man with no phone and no name. The doubts are making her irritable, even angry. Her time has been wasted on a schoolgirl fantasy. Like there's nothing else she could be doing. Like she doesn't have her own problems. Not that Gypsy would ever think to ask. Aleah feels herself on the cusp of saying something she might regret. *Time for a pause,* she thinks.

"I have to use the bathroom," she tells Gypsy. "When I get back, we should probably go."

She hurries away before Gypsy can object. In the parlor's private bathroom, she runs water over her wrists while she talks to herself in the mirror.

You're here for Gypsy, she tells herself. *Gypsy believes this is real. She needs to believe this is real.*

But then, she thinks, *so what? What has any of it got to do with me?*

For the first time, Aleah wonders if she might have mistaken pity for friendship.

Stop it, she tells herself. *You're just tired and cranky. Tomorrow, you won't think like this anymore.*

But for now, the best she can do is put on a brave face. She leaves the bathroom feeling no better or worse than before.

On her way back to the booth, she sees someone sitting with Gypsy. She feels her mood change: the world is once again a kind place. She's never been so happy to be wrong. Gypsy has someone. She actually has someone. But then Aleah sees who it is sitting there — not Gypsy's Secret Sam, but her mother. Aleah considers running out the door but makes herself walk forward. Dee Dee looks up at her, smiles.

"I'll take Gypsy home," she says.

Aleah is flustered.

"Are you sure?" she asks. "I mean, I was . . ."

Dee Dee stands, looms over her. Aleah is

keenly aware of heads turning across the parlor.

"Listen to me, Aleah Martin," Dee Dee says. "You stay the hell away from my daughter. That girl don't know the difference between what's real and what's made up in her head. You think you're helping, but you're hurting. So you just find some other way to earn your Girl Scout badge. Gypsy's off-limits. You hear what I'm saying?"

Aleah nods. She catches a glimpse of Gypsy huddled behind her mother's plus-size frame, her head hanging low. She doesn't bother to say goodbye.

Outside, her fists clenched and her face burning red, Aleah thinks, *Good riddance.* Almost instantly, she hates herself for having the thought.

CHAPTER 19

Gypsy feels a jolt in her spine as Dee Dee drives her wheelchair hard over a crack in the concrete.

"I always knew you to be ungrateful, but this tops it all," Dee Dee says. "You'll be lucky if I don't take the belt to your behind when we get home. If you're healthy enough to go tramping around, then you're healthy enough for the damn switch."

Dee Dee is shouting in plain view and earshot of pedestrians and passing cars. Gypsy keeps her head down, prays that her mother did not park too far away. Luckily, it is after nine p.m. on a weeknight in a sleepy town, with only a handful of restaurants and bars open. Her greatest fear is that Nicholas will choose this moment to appear — that he will witness her being rocketed down a public street by her out-of-control mother. She feels, more clearly than ever, ashamed of the picture she and her mother make. Ashamed of her mother's obesity. Ashamed of her own ailments and handicaps, most of which — maybe all of which — she doesn't understand. She wishes she could disappear — simply dissolve, like in *Star Trek,* and resurface somewhere entirely different. Someplace tropical, maybe. A jungle lined with beaches. Sun shining year round on exotic plants and animals. She would swim and hike and draw and paint, and she wouldn't care if she never saw another human being in her life.

Meanwhile, Dee Dee is beside herself with the kind of anger that won't die down until she's tired herself out.

"I thought you cleared your system of this kind of stupidity down in Naples," she says. "I just don't know how to get through to you. I truly don't. Tonight, I want you to park yourself in front of a mirror and take a good hard look. You ain't like other people, Gypsy. Not even a little bit. You need looking after, and won't no one but me do it."

They turn onto a side street, and Gypsy spots their car parked with one wheel on the curb at the end of the block.

"There are times you're too weak to lift a spoon," Dee Dee goes on. "Times you can't hardly wipe your own ass. I've scrubbed vomit from your clothes, washed your sheets

331

in the dead of night when you pissed yourself like a small child. Now who the hell's gonna sign up for that if they don't have to?"

She opens the passenger door and steps back while Gypsy, hands gripping the hood, lifts herself from the wheelchair into the car. A few minutes later they are jetting down residential streets, Dee Dee aggressively slamming on the brakes at every stop sign.

"I bet you're wondering how I tracked you down tonight," she says. "Well, I went into your computer and took a long look around. Turns out you've gotten real sloppy about covering your tracks. Anyway, I set Mr. Godejohn good and straight. Let him know how many laws he'd be breaking if he showed up at that parlor. You won't be hearing from him again."

Gypsy suppresses a little whimper.

"And by the way," Dee Dee says, "don't go thinking you got a computer no more. It's boxed up already. This is a new day, little missy. The rules are the same, but the consequences just got real consequential."

Gypsy is too numb to cry. She feels humiliated not by her mother's tirade, not by the scene her mother made in front of Aleah, but rather by her earlier misguided belief that she might just get away with it, that she might manage to behave in the world the way other people behaved. She understands now that her future will look no different than her present. This is her life, here in this car.

"You listening to me?" Dee Dee says. "Speak when you're spoken to."

"Yes, Mama."

Yes to all of it, Gypsy thinks. *Yes to everything you say. This is me surrendering. Once and for all.*

A half-hour later, Gypsy is lying in bed when Dee Dee, who has dropped her screaming in favor of the silent treatment, brings in a cup of water and the nightly cocktail of meds. She sets them on the side table, then turns and walks out, slamming the door behind her.

This time, without her mother watching, Gypsy sits up straight and swallows every last pill.

CHAPTER 20

Slater sits across the table from Nicholas Godejohn in a bare and forbidding concrete-and-tile interrogation room. They've dressed Nicholas in an orange jumpsuit. His dark hair is matted and oily; his morning breath has only grown more rank over the past few hours. He is skinny, short, pale. *Sickly,* Slater thinks. He might even pass for Gypsy's brother.

"I confessed," Godejohn says. "What more we got to talk about?"

"Quite a bit," Slater says. "The judge and the lawyers and the jury will want the full picture. They'll want details. A timeline."

"What kind of details?"

"Every kind. They'll want your every thought and action from the moment you met Gypsy to the moment we slapped the cuffs on."

"First of all," Nicholas says, "I never knew she was called Gypsy Rose till you all told me. She said her name was Penelope. People shouldn't be allowed to make up fake names on a Christian dating site."

Slater sees already where this is going: Godejohn will make himself an accomplice — a victim of Gypsy's siren spell.

"You've been arrested before," Slater pivots.

"Now don't go bringing that up," Nicholas says. "That was a big mix-up and it ain't got nothing to do with this."

Slater ignores him.

"For public lewdness," he continues. "Apparently, you were watching porn and giving yourself a yank in the middle of a fast food restaurant at three thirty in the afternoon. Around the time school kids would be showing up."

"You got it wrong. It wasn't like they say. Not one bit."

"How was it, then?"

"First off, I had a jacket over my lap, so no one saw nothing worth seeing. And I was sitting far off in a corner by myself. No way no one but me saw that screen."

"Someone must have seen it."

"Yeah, well . . . that someone must've tried real hard."

Slater decides to change tacks.

"No need to be defensive, Nick," he says.

"If anything, I think your prior helps you."

"Yeah, right. How's that gonna help me?"

"It shows your emotional state. The jury will read it as a cry for help. You must have been very lonely. You belonged in therapy, not prison. In fact, if they'd got you the help you needed, Dee Dee Blancharde might still be alive."

"You mean then it ain't my fault?"

"It's less your fault."

Nick looks disappointed.

"Yeah, OK," he says.

"And I'm guessing that same loneliness led you to Christian Couples?"

"Ain't no other reason to go on there. I mean, a guy's got to be pretty hard up to start shopping for strangers online."

"I know that's true," Slater says. "Hell, I've been there myself."

"Yeah, huh?"

"I'd been divorced ten years and hadn't so much as touched a woman in all that time. Unless you count prostitution busts."

Godejohn smiles.

"It'd been a while for me, too. I ain't even gonna say how long."

"What led you to Christian Couples?"

"They got a billboard up on the highway. Says something about God being the first matchmaker on account of Adam and Eve."

336

Slater knows that billboard. It stands maybe fifty yards from an adult store for swingers.

"How long ago did you join?" he asks.

"Not long before I met Penelope . . . I mean Gypsy."

"Did you meet anyone besides Gypsy?"

"Not to speak of. Just some chat room flirting that didn't go nowhere."

Slater smiles. He has Godejohn a little more relaxed, a little more trusting. It's time, he thinks, to dig in.

"So why Gypsy? What made her different?"

Godejohn shrugs. His eyes dart around the room.

"She was the only one," he says.

"The only one?"

"Who reached out to me. She clicked the Like button on my photo. Even sent me a little note 'bout how cute I was. I didn't have to do no chasing at all."

Good, Slater thinks. *We can check on that.* This is the real purpose of the interview: solicit statements that might support or contradict Godejohn's version of events.

"And she kept on pursuing you?" he asks.

"Oh yeah. You wouldn't know it to look at her, but that one's pure vixen."

He tells Slater about the midnight cos-

337

play, goes into great detail about the fantasies — all of them, he claims, Gypsy's — that had them dressed as pirate and princess, shepherd and shepherdess, sorcerer and sorceress, alien and astronaut.

"At first, I took it personal," he says. "I thought she just didn't wanna see my face unless there was some kind of mask on it. But it turns out that's her thing. It's cosplay or the highway with her. Hell, she might even like jail. She might never want to leave. It's all costumes in there."

Salter takes a sip of coffee while he thinks through his next question: "Now, this is very important, Nicholas," he begins. "Did Gypsy always know she could walk? Did she know from the start that she wasn't sick?"

Godejohn squirms a little in his seat.

"Well, I wouldn't say from the start."

"When did she know?"

"I ain't sure, exactly. You kinda gotta read between the lines with Gypsy."

"Tell me more."

"Well, she kept going on about someone she called the Savior. Took me a while to figure out that the Savior was some kind a doctor. She'd write things like: *The Savior says I'm fit to walk on water,* and *The Savior says my blood's the same as everyone else's. He says I can sleep just by closing my eyes.*

338

And then I had to figure out that her ma was the one she called the Lard Monster. The Lard Monster tied her to chairs and wouldn't let her eat nothing. The Lard Monster shaved off all her hair before it had a chance to grow. The Lard Monster did this and that and the other, all of them things the devil himself couldn't make no worse."

Slater nods as though something has clicked into place.

"So the Lard Monster had to die?" he says.

"After a while, yeah. Maybe Gypsy had that in mind the whole time. You'd have to ask her."

"Here's what I really want to know," Slater says. "How is it that you wound up with the knife in your hand?"

Nicholas thinks back to that night. He sees himself lingering at the curb, his heart beating so hard he can barely hear over it. He must have spent an hour just staring at the dark house. Then came the slow walk up the steps to the Blanchardes' front door. He found it unlocked, just as Gypsy promised.

"I don't know," he says. "It was like we were playing one of our games, only in real life. Gypsy needed saving."

"And you'd never met her before? I mean in person."

"No sir."

"But she knew what you were going to do?"

"I'm tellin' you, it was her idea. From start to finish."

Slater rubs his thumbs hard against his temples.

"You're saying you went over there to kill the mother of a young woman you'd never so much as laid eyes on?"

Nicholas grins, nods enthusiastically. As though he's found his defense. As though the fact that he'd never seen Gypsy in the flesh makes his actions selfless. Chivalric. Knight Nicholas Godejohn riding to the damsel's rescue.

CHAPTER 21

Slater and Dr. Ryan watch through a two-way mirror as Draper interrogates Gypsy. Dr. Ryan, for his part, marvels at how far Gypsy's physical transformation has progressed in such a short period of time. Her hair is crew-cut length now. Her cheeks have some color, and there's already a bit more meat on her bones. Despite her predicament, she looks healthy — probably for the first time in her life.

There's a laptop sitting open on the table between Gypsy and Draper.

"I want to play something for you," Draper says, angling the screen in Gypsy's direction.

"All right," Gypsy says.

Draper presses Play. It's a clip from Gypsy's appearance on *Mornings with Anne-Marie,* the moment when she claims that she and her mother are "like the same person . . . two peas in a pod." They finish each other's thoughts, are stronger together than they could ever be apart. When the segment is done, Draper spins the laptop back around, hits Stop.

"That was just a short while ago," Draper says. "Were you lying?"

"No."

"When did it become a lie?"

"It didn't."

"Really?" Draper asks, unconvinced. "Let me show you something else."

She calls up a screenshot from Gypsy's Christian Couples account, begins reading aloud from a series of messages between Gypsy and Nicholas, reading only Gypsy's part:

"It's [The *it* here is your mother.] *got $4,000 in a safe and I know the combination . . . Once it takes its sleep meds it don't wake for nothing . . . Better make that an extra-long knife. LOL! Ha ha ha! . . . I'll be sure the door ain't locked."*

Draper snaps the laptop shut.

"There's no doubt that you were the mastermind, Gypsy," she says. "The point of my talking to you today isn't to get a confession. We don't need one. This is your chance to explain *why*. Get your story on record. How did you go from that interview with Anne-Marie to killing your mother just a few months later? What happened?"

Gypsy looks everywhere but at Draper.

"I learned some things," she says.

"You mean about your illness?"

"I ain't ill. That's what I learned. It was her making me ill."

"Since when?"

"Since always. Since before I can remember. 'Cause I can't remember no time when I was normal. When I could eat what other people ate. When I didn't have tubes sticking out of me. When I had hair. When I had all my teeth and none of them was cracked or crumbling. When I could see right. When I could walk. And then I find out that I could've been normal the whole time. I could've gone to school. I could've had friends."

"But you can walk now," Draper says. "Why didn't you just walk away? Walk somewhere and tell someone?"

"It ain't that easy."

"Why not? Pretend I'm sitting on your jury. Make me understand."

Gypsy bangs her open palms on the table. For the first time, she raises her voice, looks Draper straight in the eyes.

"Where were you people before? How come what I did is a crime and what she did ain't?"

"Maybe it was a crime," Draper says. "We didn't know."

"Yeah, well I didn't know neither."

"But how is that possible? How can you have two perfectly healthy legs and not know it?"

"Cause no one told me different. From when I was a baby. It was always just her telling me things."

"What kinds of things?"

"That I had defects in my chromosomes. That my own blood was trying to kill me. That real food was like poison to someone sick as me. That it was just her saving my life day in and out and wouldn't nobody else ever want the job. That my brain was weak on account of everything else wrong with me. That I'd never get hired to do nothing 'cause there wasn't nothing I could do as good as other people. That my legs was born dead and we might as well cut 'em off for all the good they did me. That I'd better pray the end came for me before it came for her or I'd find out what this world was really about."

Draper listens, struggles to maintain a neutral expression. Whether or not Gypsy is telling the truth, the scope of what can go wrong between two people — between a mother and daughter — has stretched

344

beyond the bounds of her imagination. She's beginning to understand why Slater is so jaded.

"And you believed all of that?" she asks.

"I told you — no one gave me nothing else to believe."

"So what changed, Gypsy? Was it Katrina? Moving here?"

"I been thinking on that ever since Mama died. Moving here sped things up, but really it started with that trip we took last year."

She tells Draper about her encounter with Robert, the fake bionic man.

"Maybe he was a deviant, like my mama said. But then maybe he wasn't. I started thinking that maybe what happened down there could happen again. And again and again. As many times as I wanted. And if that was true, then a lot of what my mama said just couldn't be. I think I half knew it already — I just didn't know where to start looking for the truth. There were so many lies. Nothing but lies. Then we moved here and met Pastor Mike."

"Was it Pastor Mike who helped you understand that you weren't sick?"

"Yeah, but he didn't mean to be helpful that way. He was like a new audience for my mama, and I could see him believing every word out of her mouth without asking no questions. She could've said anything and he would've believed her. She could've told him I was part giraffe and he wouldn't have batted an eye. And then I could see he felt sorry for her. For *her*, not me. And he's a grown man. That made me mad in a way I ain't never been mad before. And that's why I went on that site. 'Cause I wanted to prove to him and her and myself that Robert the bionic deviant wasn't the only one in this wide world who could want me. There had to be other Roberts out there, and some of 'em had to be good people. That's just math."

"So when you opened your Christian Couples account you still didn't know for sure that you could walk? That you could eat solid food? That you could grow your hair as long as you like?"

"No, ma'am. That all came later."

"When?"

"When that doctor told me to stand up in his office and I did it and then I saw Mama's face. Her face told it all. The whole story."

On the other side of the two-way mirror, Slater turns to Dr. Ryan, raises an eyebrow.

"I guess that would be you," he says.

"I guess it would."

346

CHAPTER 22

"Munchausen syndrome by Proxy," Dr. Ryan says.

"What now?" Slater asks.

"It's a kind of mental illness. Dee Dee forced Gypsy to pretend she was sick. More than that, she tricked Gypsy into *believing* she was sick. Although 'tricked' may not be the right word. Chances are Dee Dee believed in Gypsy's illness, too."

"So you're saying it's Dee Dee who was mentally ill?"

"In so many words, yes."

"How does that happen? What kind of misfire in the brain makes a mother hurt her own child?"

Dr. Ryan shrugs.

"Dee Dee didn't think she was hurting Gypsy," he says. "Quite the opposite. People break with reality when it isn't meeting their needs."

"That sounds awfully convenient. What

347

was it Dee Dee Blancharde needed?"

"If I had to guess, I'd say security. Emotional security. I'm willing to bet she didn't have any in her own childhood. She turned Gypsy into someone who couldn't function without her. Someone who could never leave her. A lifetime of guaranteed love."

Slater sniggers.

"She managed to squeeze a new house out of it, too. And a lot of swell trips. Not to mention the four grand Gypsy and Godejohn made off with."

"That's just part of the disease," Dr. Ryan says. "The world owes me, so I won't be shy about taking."

Draper, who'd left to give Gypsy a short rest, is back now carrying two bottles of water and a bag of chips. She pulls open the bag, holds it out to Gypsy.

"Since you can now," she says.

The gaps between Gypsy's front teeth become painfully obvious when she chews.

"I want to talk about that night," Draper says.

"You mean the night Mama died?"

"I mean the night she was murdered."

Gypsy looks startled.

"Murdered? It was self-defense," she says.

"No, it wasn't. We need to be clear about that."

"You don't think she would've killed me the way we was going? Look at me. I took on ten pounds already and still I look like this."

She holds her rail-thin arms out to the sides for Draper to examine.

"I understand," Draper says. "But the problem is, you didn't need to kill her to make yourself safe."

Draper is trying to draw out some sign of remorse or responsibility — anything that might sit well with a jury.

"But I didn't kill her," Gypsy says. "Nicholas did that."

"He held the knife, but you —"

"I was screaming for him to stop. Once he started, I didn't want it no more. Mama, she didn't hardly make no noise at all, but I was screaming so loud Nicholas just about ran out of the house. I loved my mama. I know that sounds crazy now, but I did. I loved her. I still do."

Draper takes a long breath.

"So why did you let Nicholas into your home to kill her? I know you must have been angry. You must have —"

"It wasn't 'cause I was angry. I mean, I was, but that wasn't it."

"What was it, then?"

"I didn't see no other way."

Gypsy reaches absently for the bag of chips, then pulls her hand away.

"I had this idea," she says, "that I'd never be OK while Mama was still alive. I couldn't just leave."

"Because she'd find you?"

"That was part of it. She found me in Florida. But it wasn't just that. It was like — I couldn't undo what she done to me by myself. Someone who wasn't me had done all these things to me, and I needed someone who wasn't me to set it all right."

Draper works to hide her confusion.

"You're talking about revenge?" she asks.

"No, I ain't. I . . . how was I supposed to know the whole world wasn't like Mama? How was I supposed to run off if I didn't know what I was running to? And Nicholas said he'd look after me. He was gonna take me with him to Canada. We were gonna live up in the mountains and he was gonna teach me to fish and hunt and ski. I hadn't ever walked before, but now I was gonna ski down a mountain."

"I understand," Draper says.

She leans back, takes a quick drink of water. She feels suddenly as though she could sleep for days on end.

Outside the room, Dr. Ryan turns back to Slater.

"She wasn't just leaving her mother," he says. "She was leaving a universe. A universe that included just one other person. She couldn't imagine that world going on without her."

"So now you're a shrink?" Slater asks.

"Just an observer," Dr. Ryan says.

They go back to watching the interview.

"What's gonna happen to me now?" Gypsy asks.

"That's up to the judge and jury."

"But what about *now*?"

"You'll have to wait for your trial in jail."

"But they can't do nothing too bad to me, right? On account of my age."

"What do you mean?" Draper asks.

"I mean I ain't an adult yet, so they can't lock me up for real."

"But you're . . ."

And then Draper understands.

"Gypsy," she says, "how old do you think you are?"

Gypsy rolls her eyes.

"I know how old I am," she says. "Fifteen next month."

"Gypsy," Draper says, "we have a copy of your birth certificate. You're nineteen years old."

Gypsy giggles a little, then turns serious as this final lie sinks in.

351

"Jesus Christ," Slater says.

"Now are you convinced?" Dr. Ryan asks. "That girl has lived her whole life in an alternative reality. She doesn't know this world that you and I live in."

"Well," Slater says, "prison should get her up to speed."

"You think she deserves that?" Dr. Ryan asks.

Slater shrugs.

"I think it isn't up to me."

CHAPTER 23

After a month-long trial, it took the jury just a few hours to find Gypsy guilty. Now she is back in court for sentencing. She sits with her state-appointed lawyer at the defendant's table. Aleah, sitting just a few feet away in the front row, hardly recognizes the friend she'd spent so much time with. In place of her ridiculous hat with the dangling pompoms, Gypsy has a full head of spiky black hair. Her posture is straight and strong. No oxygen tank, no tubes, no wheelchair. And her clothes — even her orange prison jumpsuit — no longer hang off her body like drapery.

The bailiff demands the room's attention as Judge Raymond Parnell takes his seat. He is past middle age but still young for a judge, with close-cropped salt-and-pepper hair and very fine, almost feminine hands. He does not smile, does not so much as glance at Gypsy or make eye contact with anyone in the court. Instead, he slips on a pair of glasses, takes up a single sheet of paper, and begins reading. Gypsy remains motionless. Aleah shuts her eyes, listens.

There is a brief preamble concerning the facts of the case and the options available to the court before Judge Parnell arrives at his decision: "In light of the long history of abuse endured by the defendant at the hands of the deceased," he begins, "in light of the sequestration, if not downright imprisonment, that robbed her of anything resembling a proper childhood, and in light of the legitimate if misguided fear she undoubtedly felt for her own life, it is the ruling of this court that Gypsy Rose Blancharde shall serve the minimum sentence permitted by law, which is to say no more than ten years and no fewer than seven."

Aleah has to clasp her hands over her mouth to keep from cheering. There are tears in her eyes, but when she looks at Gypsy she sees nothing: no joy, no anger, no sadness. Not even resignation.

A female bailiff signals for Gypsy to stand, then cuffs her hands behind her back and begins to lead her from the courtroom. They are within inches of Aleah before Gypsy spots her friend. She smiles, and Aleah notices for the first time that Gypsy has been fitted with new teeth.

"Can I get just a second?" Gypsy asks. The bailiff nods, takes a single step back. Gypsy turns toward Aleah.

"It's real good of you to come," she says. "I ain't seen you in a while. You been all right?"

Her voice is lower-pitched and more relaxed than Aleah remembers.

"Who cares how am I?" Aleah says. "How are you? That's good news you got today. At least, compared to what it could have been."

Gypsy starts to answer, then sees that Aleah is crying, or maybe trying hard not to.

"What's wrong?" she asks.

"It's just . . . I don't know. I miss you. I wish you could come home now. And I feel . . . God, I'm so sorry, Gypsy. I had no idea. If I'd known —"

"It's OK, Aleah," Gypsy says. "It's all OK."

"But how? How can it be OK?"

Gypsy smiles.

"I'm at peace now," she says. "I'm freer than I've ever been in my whole life."

"Yeah," Aleah says. "I guess you are."

She leans forward, gives Gypsy a quick peck on the cheek.

"We'll go paddle boating on the lake when you're out," she says. "The two of us. And I'll teach you to drive."

The bailiff tugs on Gypsy's arm. Gypsy looks over her shoulder as they walk off.

"I hope to God you're far away from here by then," she says. "But wherever you are, I promise I'll come visit."

ABOUT THE AUTHOR

James Patterson holds the Guinness World Record for the most #1 *New York Times* bestsellers. His books have sold more than 355 million copies worldwide. He has donated more than one million books to students and soldiers and has over four hundred Teacher Education Scholarships at twenty-four colleges and universities. He has also donated millions to independent bookstores and school libraries.

The employees of Thorndike Press hope you have enjoyed this Large Print book. All our Thorndike, Wheeler, and Kennebec Large Print titles are designed for easy reading, and all our books are made to last. Other Thorndike Press Large Print books are available at your library, through selected bookstores, or directly from us.

For information about titles, please call:
(800) 223-1244

or visit our website at:
gale.com/thorndike

To share your comments, please write:
Publisher
Thorndike Press
10 Water St., Suite 310
Waterville, ME 04901